GUIDE TO COURT REFORM AND THE ROLE OF COURT PERSONNEL

A GUIDE FOR USAID DEMOCRACY AND GOVERNANCE WORKERS

JULY 2009

PREFACE

This manual provides practical guidance on successful court personnel and management reform projects. Using this manual, rule of law officers can make better-informed decisions about court personnel system improvement interventions; oversee the design of programs that achieve results; and ensure and plan, to the extent possible, for long-term sustainability that enables these programs to enhance the rule of law.

Comments regarding this publication and inquiries regarding programming for court personnel reform should be directed to:

Keith Crawford
Rule of Law Division
Tel: (202) 712-1471
Fax: (202) 216-3231
kcrawford@usaid.gov

Office of Democracy and Governance
Bureau for Democracy, Conflict, and Humanitarian Assistance
U.S. Agency for International Development
Washington, D.C. 20523-3100

More information, including electronic versions of the center's Technical Publication Series, is available from the center's Intranet site at http://inside.usaid.gov/G/DG/ and USAID's democracy Internet site at http://www.usaid.gov/our_work/democracy_and_governance/publications/.

American Bar Association Rule of Law Initiative

The American Bar Association (ABA) Rule of Law Initiative promotes legal reform efforts in over 40 countries in Africa, Asia, Central and Eastern Europe, Latin America, the Caribbean, the Middle East, and North Africa. It traces its origins to 1990, with the creation of the ABA's Central European and Eurasian Law Initiative (CEELI) and the opening of its first overseas office in Sofia, Bulgaria, in 1991. The ABA launched sister initiatives in Asia in 1998, and in Africa, Latin America, and the Caribbean in 2000. In 2003, the ABA launched its Middle East program. In 2006, these regional programs were consolidated into a single entity now known as the ABA Rule of Law Initiative.

Today, the Rule of Law Initiative has approximately 500 professional staff working in the United States and abroad, including a cadre of short- and long-term expatriate volunteers who typically spend from three months to two years in the field providing technical assistance.

The Rule of Law Initiative's work in the field is supported by the Research and Program Development (RPD) Office which is composed of a team of lawyers based in the Initiative's headquarters in Washington, D.C. The RPD Office develops and implements a series of highly regarded assessment tools, provides in-depth assessments of draft legislation at the request of host country partners, conducts legal research, and produces a variety of papers and resource guides on rule of law issues. To date, the RPD Office has developed assessment tools in the following areas: Judicial Reform, Legal Profession Reform, Prosecutorial Reform, Legal Education Reform, Human Trafficking, Human Rights, and Women's Rights.

GUIDE TO COURT REFORM AND THE ROLE OF COURT PERSONNEL

A GUIDE FOR USAID DEMOCRACY AND GOVERNANCE WORKERS

JULY 2009

ACKNOWLEDGMENTS

Barry Walsh

Barry Walsh served as the primary author for the *Guide to Court Reform and the Role of Court Personnel*. Mr. Walsh is an international justice and court systems consultant and former senior court administrator in state and federal court systems in Australia. He has managed and advised on public sector management and court administration for over 20 years and was the founding CEO and registrar of two specialist courts. He holds graduate qualifications in law, public sector management, and change management. His extensive international experience includes justice sector advisory work in Papua New Guinea, Nepal, India, Indonesia, Bangladesh, Afghanistan, the Philippines, Oman, Macedonia, Egypt, and Colombia.

Scott Lyons

Scott Lyons served as the ABA Rule of Law Initiative's project coordinator, lead editor, and contributing author for the *Guide to Court Reform and the Role of Court Personnel*. Mr. Lyons holds a J.D. from American University Washington College of Law and an M.A. in international affairs from the School of International Service. He has led several judicial education projects and has worked and studied in the area of comparative law in Latin America, Asia, and Africa. Mr. Lyons currently serves as a Democracy Specialist and Anticorruption Advisor with the active component of the Civilian Response Corps at USAID. Mr. Lyons' dedication to this project was instrumental to the successful completion of the guide and is particularly appreciated.

Advisory Group

An advisory group reviewed guide drafts and recommended numerous structural and content improvements. Members of the group included Russell Wheeler, former Deputy Director of the U.S. Federal Judicial Center (FJC) and current guest scholar at the Brookings Institution; Mira Gur-Arie, Director, Interjudicial Relations Office of the U.S. Federal Judicial Center (FJC); Kurt Riechenberg, Legal Secretary for the Court of Justice of the European Communities and Secretary of the Group of Wise Persons established by the Ministers of the Council of Europe for the purpose of making suggestions for reforming the European Court of Human Rights; Judge Larry Eisenhauer, Iowa Court of Appeals; Dory Reiling, Judge and Senior Judicial Reform Expert for the Justice Reform Practice Group at the Legal Vice President's Office of the World Bank; and Linn Hammergren, Senior Public Sector Management Specialist in the World Bank Latin America regional department, working in the areas of judicial reform and anti-corruption.

We are especially indebted to Markus Zimmer and Dr. Andrew Cannon, who each reviewed advance drafts and offered detailed suggestions for improvements and drafting language. Markus Zimmer, a member of the advisory group, is the founding president of the International Association for Court Administration and a former senior court clerk/administrator of the U.S. District Court of Utah. He has worked with numerous USAID rule of law projects in Europe, Asia, Africa, and the Middle East. Dr. Cannon is Deputy Chief Magistrate of the state of South Australia and author of articles on law and jurisprudence.

Many people contributed to the development of the guide, including Simon Conté, Wendy Patten, Ebony Wade, Brenner Allen, and Diana Okoeva. The ABA would also like to recognize Eve Epstein for her role in conducting the final edits and producing the final draft.

CONTENTS

EXECUTIVE SUMMARY

The purpose of this guide is to assist USAID democracy and governance (DG) officers and contractors in designing and implementing rule of law reform initiatives that improve court personnel and court management. This guide defines court personnel as both judges and non-judicial staff who work in the court and enable it to carry out its functions. The guide is practical and realistic. It provides an overview of the operational aspects of court systems, focusing on the judicial and non-judicial personnel whose functions are essential to the effective administration of justice in all types of legal systems. It also describes how court personnel can be organized, managed, developed, and used most effectively to ensure that courts deliver justice competently and foster public confidence.

USAID's publication of this guide reflects how the rule of law development community has modified its assumptions and strategies in the pursuit of strategic court system reform. The earlier, almost exclusive focus on strengthening judiciaries through significant investment in the education, training, professional development, and political organization of judges has shifted. Reform efforts now target the broader institutional framework within which judicial activity occurs. They distribute resources more evenly throughout the organizational functions that contribute to achieving more effective courts and higher standards of justice. Greater professional development and strategic use of non-judicial court staff have high potential to increase productivity, improve transparency, and enhance public service and external relations.

Chapter I describes the guide's purpose, its application to rule of law programs, how it was developed, and its unique contribution to advancing court administration reform.

Chapter II defines the range of legal systems that exist throughout the world. It also describes key differences among systems, four features of these systems, and how these features affect the use of court personnel. The four features are: (1) structure and organization of judiciaries, (2) the methods and principles courts use to conduct hearings and decide cases, (3) participants in the adjudication process, and (4) judicial independence and separation of powers.

Chapter III focuses on court personnel management, first at the judicial system level and then at the individual court level. It describes two opposing national models: (1) the Justice Ministry Model, in which the executive branch, frequently a Ministry of Justice, controls the judicial system's administrative and budgetary functions; and (2) the Separate Branch Model, in which the judiciary self-governs and exercises budgetary control of judicial system operations. In this context, it highlights issues, trends, and mechanisms related to increasing self-governance. At the individual court level, it describes three management models: (1) judicial management by a chief judge, (2) judicial cadre management where several judges hold management positions, and (3) professional court management by non-judicial personnel. Recent trends that shift non-judicial management and administrative responsibilities from chief judges to professional court managers are significant because they release chief judges from frequently burdensome administrative responsibilities, allowing them to focus on court leadership and the professional development of junior-level judges.

Chapter IV describes how court personnel support core court functions. It defines nine phases of case adjudication, beginning with case initiation and ending with enforcement of the judgment, and shows the role of non-judicial personnel in each phase.

Chapter V provides guidance in rule of law programming that targets the reform of court management and personnel. It begins with program principles and strategies, highlighting the critical need for early and continued buy-in from leaders of the executive, legislative, and judicial branches as well as other stakeholders. It then describes three components of court reform programming that can improve court management and personnel, along with best practice interventions in each component. The components are (1) strategic policy reform, (2) skills and knowledge development, and (3) court business, court systems, and infrastructure reform. Key recommendations and best practices set forth in this chapter include:

- Addressing strategic policy reform by facilitating the development of national strategies for managerial reform of the court system, supporting legislative reform related to court processes, and improving the funding, governance, and structure of the court system

- Supporting training that is needs-based, is an appropriate solution to critical court system problems, strengthens local training institutions, and reaches both judges and non-judicial court personnel

- Implementing a variety of business information tools to increase the competence of court personnel

- Harnessing the power of information technology to transform and expand access to court case information and performance statistics

- Using pilot courts to test new processes, procedures, and information technology applications

- Building a professional cadre of court personnel through transparent performance management, enforceable standards of conduct, and merit-based promotions

I. INTRODUCTION: COURT REFORM AND THE ROLE OF COURT PERSONNEL

> *The importance of administration as something demanding the highest genius, and not something for underpaid clerks, must be enforced by precept and example—in all contexts.*
>
> —Professor Jacques Barzun of Columbia University, 1973

Purpose of this guide. The purpose of this guide is to assist USAID democracy and governance (DG) officers and contractors in designing and implementing initiatives that improve court personnel and court management. USAID has developed several publications that enable the agency to reach missions and other audiences more effectively with the latest technical knowledge in the field of democracy and governance. This guide advances that work by focusing on court personnel and the range of systems these personnel use to manage courts. In this guide, court personnel includes both judges and non-judicial staff.

The importance of court personnel and management reform in rule of law programs. Court personnel are an integral component of successful rule of law reform because they are essential for the efficient, effective, and transparent administration of justice. They implement the management reforms that underlie the administration of justice.

In many states with weak or newly emerging democratic traditions, existing laws are inequitable or inequitably applied, judicial independence is compromised, individual and minority rights are not guaranteed, and institutions lack the capacity to administer existing laws. Weak legal institutions endanger democratic reform and sustainable development. Reform of court personnel and court management is an essential component in addressing these concerns. Court personnel functions are vital to court operations; without improving personnel competencies, courts are hard pressed to meet citizens' needs. Regardless of the type of government, the changing world economy requires that courts be able to resolve increasingly complex cases. These demands place a continuous

RULE OF LAW

The "rule of law"... refers to a principle of governance in which all persons, institutions and entities, public and private, including the State itself, are accountable to laws that are publicly promulgated, equally enforced and independently adjudicated, and which are consistent with international human rights norms and standards.[1]

burden on judiciaries to enhance and develop their personnel resources.

USAID justice sector programs. A large component of USAID's justice sector programming focuses on judicial development and facilitating the emergence of independent and robust judiciaries. USAID's experience has shown that success in judicial system reform requires much more than developing judges as individual adjudicators; it also requires attention to the broader managerial systems and organizational structures of courts, including the personnel employed to sustain them. This guide examines those systems, structures, and personnel. It also offers guidance on how donor-assisted rule of law programs can develop them.

Goals of rule of law programs. The general goals of rule of law programs are to improve the administration of justice and to increase citizen access to responsive and efficient justice. Court personnel and management reform is an emerging focal point of USAID's democracy and good governance goals. Successful reform has a positive impact on the rule of law, human rights, anti-corruption, and accountability among government institutions. Further, court personnel and management reform is one component of improving a government's ability to maintain civil order, guarantee the rule of law, and promote economic growth.

How the guide was developed. Five activities contributed to the development of this guide:

(1)   Site visits to the Philippines, Macedonia, Egypt, Colombia, and South Africa in mid-2006 and the preparation of a case study on judicial system reform developments in each country

(2)   Review of similar judicial reform projects in Mongolia and Russia

---

[1]United Nations Security Council: The Rule of Law and Transitional Justice in Conflict and Post Conflict Societies. Report of the Secretary General. 3 August 2004, page 4, paragraph 6.

(3)   Consolidation of the experience and expertise of the principal author, lead editor, and advisory experts in court management and court reform

(4)   A desk study of the relevant literature

(5)   Analysis of the case studies and the literature review to identify essential lessons, concepts, and techniques that DG officers and other rule of law program practitioners can use in improving court personnel and court management

The criteria for selecting the group of case study countries included:

(1)   Unique current court personnel programming

(2)   Regional diversity

(3)   Potential for replication on a regional and global level

(4)   Range of legal systems

(5)   Varied economic development

(6)   Use of an array of methodologies in the projects

In addition to the case studies, this guide uses several examples from the *USAID Guide for Promoting Judicial Independence and Impartiality* (January 2002).

The unique focus of this guide.
Most of the publications on international court administration reform focus on systems rather than on improving the court personnel who administer those systems. This guide is a first step in filling that gap.

How the guide is organized.
The first four chapters are descriptive, providing users with a basic understanding of courts, court personnel, and avenues for reform. The final chapter provides guidance on project implementation. The chapters are as follows:

Chapter I – Introduction: Court Reform and the Role of Court Personnel. This chapter introduces the importance of court personnel and management reform in rule of law programs and defines the purpose of the guide.

Chapter II – Court Personnel in World Legal Systems. This chapter describes world legal systems, features of these systems, and how these features affect the use of court personnel.

Chapter III – Managing Court Personnel. This chapter describes models for managing courts at the national level and the individual court level.

Chapter IV – The Use of Court Personnel in Supporting Core Court Functions. This chapter describes how court personnel, especially non-judicial personnel, support core functions of the court. It also highlights factors to consider in project design.

Chapter V – Court Personnel Reform: Project Implementation. This chapter presents general programming principles and options for project activities in strategic policy reform, skills and knowledge development, and court business, court systems, and infrastructure reforms. Like Chapter IV, it also highlights factors to consider in project design.

II. COURT PERSONNEL IN WORLD LEGAL SYSTEMS

A. ROLES OF COURT PERSONNEL

The role of judges. The primary function of courts is to resolve civil and criminal disputes through the application of law. They generally resolve these disputes through trials, where judges apply the law in their capacity as adjudicators and arbitrators. Because judges have this power, the emphasis of reform is usually to ensure that judges are competent, properly motivated, financially secure, and free of undue external influences. Courts vary tremendously in terms of size and complexity—from a temporary room with a part-time judge to an extensive set-up with hundreds of personnel and judges operating in a large urban courts complex. In a small courthouse, the judge must be able to assume all tasks necessary for the court to carry out its business. In larger and more complex courts, the judges cannot carry out all these tasks due to time and work constraints. Also, they do not necessarily have the required skills to perform certain specialized managerial tasks that complex courts require.

Therefore, in carrying out their core activities, judges work collaboratively within court organizations along with a variety of other court personnel. Consequently, for a rule of law program to influence the development of a judicial system, it must address the organizational environment in which judges operate as well as the interaction between judicial and non-judicial court personnel.

The role of non-judicial personnel. The role of non-judicial court personnel is to support the primary function of courts (resolving civil and criminal cases) and the secondary function of courts (managing court tasks that support case resolution). Courts cannot carry out their functions without these personnel, and the effectiveness and efficiency of justice is directly tied to personnel competence. The proper use of court personnel allows judges to focus on resolving cases while non-judicial staff perform essential administrative tasks.

B. WORLD LEGAL SYSTEMS

Legal systems: civil law[ll], common law, mixed, and other variations. The methods and processes that courts use are largely determined by the role the courts perform under the country's legal system. Regardless of the system, all courts share certain fundamental characteristics and goals. However, national legal systems may differ from one another in such areas as: (1) the structure and organization of the judiciary, (2) the methods and principles the courts use to conduct hearings and decide cases, (3) participants in the adjudication process, and (4) the degree to which court organizations foster and sustain their judicial independence.

Thus, in addressing court personnel and management reform, rule of law program practitioners must first identify the type of legal system and the role of the court personnel. Classifying a court system makes it easier to identify the most significant systemic deficiencies, and thus to target rule of law programming on improvements that correct those deficiencies.

The enormous variety within each type of legal system makes generalization difficult. However, practitioners need a basic understanding of the system types to understand how courts operate. This section provides that understanding.

> ### CIVIL LAW SYSTEMS
> Civil law (or code-based) describes the system of law that developed in continental Europe. It is also called European law, continental law, Roman law, Napoleonic law, or even bureaucratic law.

The most common legal systems: common law and civil law. A legal system is typically classified as either a common law system or a civil law system. However, because of variations within these systems, such a classification does not always definitively identify specific, practical characteristics of a court system.

Origins and spread of common law and civil law systems. Both systems have their origins in the law of ancient Rome that was carried across most of Europe by Roman conquerors. The civil law from most countries in continental Europe also found its way to European colonies throughout the world and, largely through the former Soviet Union, into many communist

---

[ll]"Civil law" also refers to the body of law in any country (with civil, common, or mixed law traditions) that covers essentially private rights and disputes. This body of law is distinct from the body of criminal law.

and former communist countries. The common law of England developed in its own way, in parallel with the civil law in continental Europe, and was also exported to other parts of the world as a legacy of the British Empire. Versions of civil law and common law systems are now sprinkled across countries throughout the world. However, developing countries adapted the European models and incorporated them into their own legal traditions and practices, creating wide variations from country to country.

Mixed systems. In reality, countries do not separate neatly into either civil law or common law traditions. Elements of one tradition tend to flow into the other so that in many countries, the legal system is really mixed. Scotland, for example, still retains a legal system distinct from the common law tradition in the United Kingdom. Both the U.S. (in Louisiana) and Canada (in Quebec) retain small bastions of civil law systems that operate within common law systems. Egypt has elements of common law, civil law, and Islamic law traditions.

Other legal systems. Some legal systems are called Islamic, socialist, Confucian, ecclesiastical, or military, or provide for indigenous traditions of dispute resolution. These kinds of labels can reflect either the substantive laws with which courts are concerned or the methods the courts use to interpret and apply those laws. Use of the term Islamic or Shari'a court, for example, usually indicates the types of cases handled and the law that is applied but does not indicate the methods used in the court. Indigenous systems, such as those in Africa, often use alternative dispute resolution methods that involve applying tribal principles or doctrine.

Distribution of common and civil law systems. Only a few countries—generally those where English is the dominant community or business language—have common law systems. Although most systems in the rest the world are classified as civil law, there is great variation among them. Features of the French legal system, for example, are quite different from those of the German or Italian systems. Most Latin American systems differ significantly from those of Spain or Portugal. When specialists speak of applying European practices, this can generate vigorous debate about which European alternative is preferable.

Influence of common law on civil law systems. Even though relatively few countries have common law systems, the perspectives that international donors with common law traditions bring to judicial reform programs are influential even within civil law systems. This influence is chiefly attributable to the fact that many of the successful 20th century innovations in court management and judicial systems were developed in U.S. courts and have been widely and successfully adopted by other common law and civil law systems. The influence also reflects the scale and impact of U.S.-sponsored international judicial reform programs, especially in Latin America and Central and Eastern Europe, where American expertise and experience invariably influence the range of reform options that rule of law programs foster.

C. COMMON FEATURES OF WORLD LEGAL SYSTEMS

This section describes four features of world legal systems, key differences among systems, and how these features affect the use of court personnel.

I. STRUCTURE AND ORGANIZATION OF JUDICIARIES

Appellate structures. Legal systems usually assure consistent application of the law by allowing appeals from the decisions of trial-level or first-instance courts to be adjudicated by appellate courts. Appeal rights are based on the assumption that some court decisions will be erroneous and that justice demands a routine mechanism to correct errors. The scope and sophistication of the appellate mechanism varies from one system to another. These variances are reflected in the structures of courts that are established to decide appeals. Common law systems are usually in a pyramid shape, with lower court civil and criminal decisions subject to review by a general jurisdiction appellate court. In contrast, civil law systems make greater use of specialized and other independent court structures, which frequently have separate appellate systems.

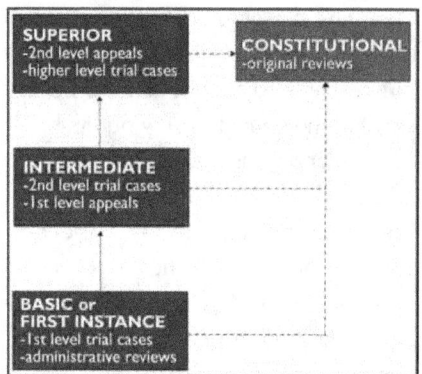

Figure I. An Example of an Appellate Court System Structure

Beyond the simple description in Figure I, there can be enormous differences from system to system. For example, some systems allow more than one appeal per case that incorporates both factual and procedural issues. Others deny appeals on facts from civil court decisions. In some cases, the decision on appeal finally determines the case, but in others, the appellate court returns the case to the lower court to complete the adjudication process. Most systems, including both civil law and common law, have two levels of appellate review: a first or intermediate level and a final level usually associated with a supreme or constitutional court. What is common in most countries is the ability of the appellate system to

ally do not extend to the supervision of judges, personnel, or administrative processes of lower courts.

Managerial structures. Most court systems are hierarchical and incorporate uniform application of rules and standards. They have a judicial chain of command that establishes policies and

the court's consideration. The main roles of judges are (1) to chair the proceedings, (2) to listen to and read the evidence, and then (3) to adjudicate. The judge is usually most directive during the pre-trial steps, when a variety of case management practices may be imposed to ensure that the trial fo-

Figure 2. The Structure of Courts in the Philippines

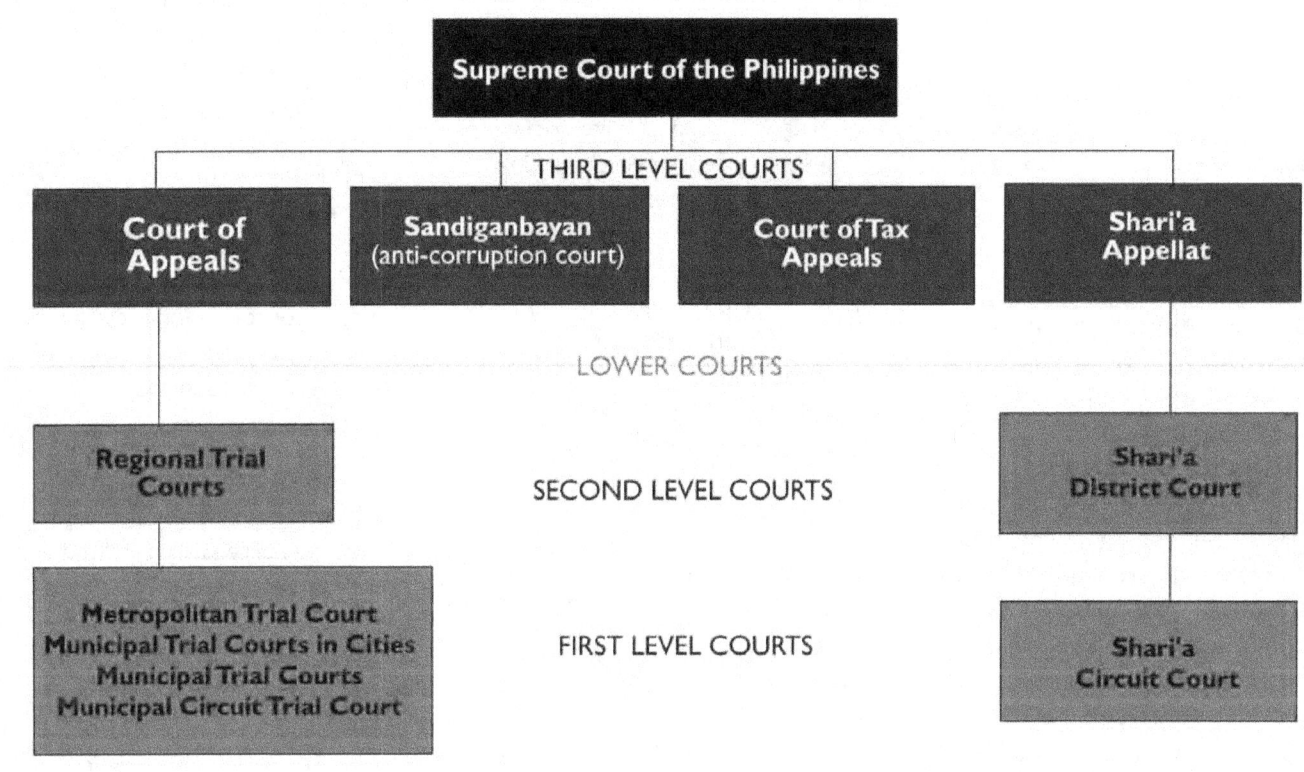

impose a degree of enforced supervision by higher courts over lower courts with respect to adjudication processes and outcomes. However, the powers of appellate courts gener-

procedures for the management and adjudicative processes of courts at each level. In the Philippines, for example, the Supreme Court is at the pinnacle of the entire court hierarchy (Figure 2).

2. THE METHODS AND PRINCIPLES COURTS USE TO CONDUCT HEARINGS AND DECIDE CASES

a. COURT PROCEDURES
Common law adversarial proceedings. In common law adversarial proceedings, courts allow advocates for the parties to define the questions in dispute and to select the evidence for

cuses on the core elements of the dispute.

Civil law inquisitorial proceedings.

The inquisitorial procedures of civil law systems are different. Two judges are usually involved at the trial level. The investigative judge conducts the investigation, compiles the evidence, and determines what evidence will be presented to the trial judge. The trial judge hears arguments, reviews evidence, and renders a decision. Since civil law judges are more active in controlling the evidentiary process, they are less reliant than common law judges on advocates and prosecutors.

Cross-fertilization between systems. Adversarial procedure and inquisitorial procedure each have strengths that courts in both common law and civil law systems often adopt. Many common law systems, for example, apply inquisitorial procedure to a range of their specialized civil courts and administrative tribunals. Similarly, many civil law systems have incorporated features of adversarial procedure into their criminal processes, which are sometimes called oral proceedings.

Oral procedure. The distinction between adversarial and inquisitorial procedure affects how evidence is compiled and presented to courts. Adversarial systems normally rely on a continuous oral trial proceeding. The focus is on preparing evidence that is usually presented orally and tested orally through cross examination. Traditionally, this entails a high degree of preparation through pre-trial steps. These steps include the exchange of written questions and answers regarding evidence that the parties intend to use at trial (called interrogatories) and formal disclosure of dispute-related docu-

---

FEATURES OF ORAL TRIALS

Evidence is presented orally with the parties present.

The parties have the opportunity to present their own evidence and to examine the evidence of the opposing party.

Judges may be required to deliberate and render their decisions immediately following the presentation of evidence at a continuous trial.

Judges promptly provide reasons for their decisions.

Appellate courts may review questions of law, though usually not facts.

---

ments to the other party (called discovery). These steps result in ascertaining evidence that may be presented and tested in the oral trial.

Inquisitorial procedure, on the other hand, also includes oral proceedings but permits judges to exercise their discretion to rely more on documentary evidence and less on oral testimony. Both inquisitorial and adversarial judges can decline to hear evidence that they believe is irrelevant or without good cause. As a result, oral proceedings can become quite brief with very little evidence being heard in open court. One weakness of document-reliant systems is that they are generally less transparent to the general public than oral procedure. Many civil law systems in Latin America and Europe have recognized this weakness in recent years, and amended their criminal law systems to introduce an oral prosecution system.

HOW NON-JUDICIAL COURT PERSONNEL SUPPORT ORAL PROCEDURES

Court personnel enable courts to offer efficient oral hearings, whether the process is adversarial or inquisitorial. They support the needs of parties by managing facilities, assisting with case management, protecting evidence, and facilitating the appearance of prisoners and witnesses. These services help avoid postponements and delays.

Appellate procedures. In some countries, intermediate and final appellate courts seldom or never conduct hearings in open court. They rely on paper processes instead of oral evidence or submissions from advocates. An example is the Supreme Court of Indonesia, which does not even have public courtrooms in its main building. The absence of any oral hearings can hinder both common law and civil law systems. Rule of law reform programs can increase the extent to which courts

use oral procedure to ensure adequate judicial control and to increase transparency.

HOW NON-JUDICIAL COURT PERSONNEL SUPPORT CONSISTENCY IN DECISION MAKING

Legally trained court staff help judges conduct thorough research and assist in drafting decisions. Other court staff ensure that decisions are properly announced and published.

---

b. CONSISTENCY IN DECISION MAKING

The importance of consistency. Court systems need to ensure that judicial decisions reflect the law and that each court decision is consistent with prior judgments of the same court as well as higher courts. Consistency is essential for promoting public confidence in the rule of law.

Common law. Judges in any legal system are obliged to apply the law, but under common law systems the principle of binding precedent also applies. Under this principle, if a law has been interpreted by a higher court, then that interpretation is ordinarily binding on judges of equivalent or lower level courts. Common law courts thereby produce what is called case law or decisional law. In the course of handing down a judgment that establishes a binding precedent, a judge often fills gaps in the law or extends or qualifies the law.

Civil law. In contrast, civil law systems usually assume that judges apply and interpret laws through their own sense of justice in each case. In theory, judges are not bound by prior decisions of other courts. In practice, however, they are expected to rule predictably, and cases with the same facts should be decided the same way. As a result, judges may be influenced by rulings of cases or authoritative directions to keep uniformity within the system. In many civil law systems, the decisions of the final court of appellate review are routinely made available to lower court judges for education and guidance.

3. PARTICIPANTS IN THE ADJUDICATION PROCESS

Single-judge or multi-judge courts. Another feature that distinguishes common law systems from civil law systems is the number of judges in the court. In common law systems, a typical trial court comprises a judge sitting alone or with a jury, although appeal courts often have three or more judges sitting together. In contrast, the civil law system courts of many Western European countries usually have a trial judge panel of three, and typically judges sit alone only for smaller claims. In most civil law systems, the adjudication of major civil and criminal cases is a joint function; minority judgments are not typical. The assumption is that the judgment will be collective and unani-

---

EXAMPLES OF FUNCTIONS PERFORMED BY JUDGES

Deciding the outcome of the case with an enforceable result.

Deciding the meaning of laws and the application of laws to the facts of the case.

Deciding the credibility of evidence and, in jury trials, instructing the jury as to how much weight to give to certain evidence.

Duties incidental to judicial functions, such as the administration of courts.[III]

---

mous. In contrast, in common law the practice of publicly announcing and publishing appellate minority judgments is the norm rather than the exception,

---

KEY ELEMENTS OF COMMON LAW JURIES

- Jury service is not voluntary. A panel of 6-14 people is empowered to determine the outcome of a particular trial. The panel is discharged once the trial is over and is not used a second time.

- The panel is drawn from the local community of the person to be tried or the plaintiff whose rights are in dispute.

- The panel determines questions of fact and sometimes questions concerning the sentence or orders that the court hands down.

- Once empanelled, and until formally discharged, jury members cannot have contact with the parties or their legal counsel in the case, or with the presiding judges, except through the formal processes of the trial.

---

and dissenting views are considered influential. In common law systems, diversity of opinion is thought to ensure the quality of judicial decisions.

The role of juries. Juries are a hallmark of common law systems. They evolved in early England as a check on the excesses of corrupt judges and were embraced by the American constitutional founders as a check on the prosecutorial powers of the executive branch. Juries take over the role of the presiding judge in determining the credibility of evidence and witnesses. They determine questions of fact. The presiding judge retains the exclusive power to control the processes of the trial and the interpretation of questions of law. Civil law systems generally do not give juries a central role, although in recent years Israel and Russia have introduced juries into their criminal

justice systems. In contrast, many developing common law countries abolished the jury system soon after gaining independence from common law colonial powers. These countries include the Philippines, a former American colony, and all of the former British colonies of the Indian subcontinent and Southeast Asia. In Canada, Australia, and England, jury trials have been abolished for all but a narrow range of civil disputes, though they remain a dominant element of the criminal court systems. The civil law systems did not develop juries of the English kind, largely because they tended to use at least three judges for significant trials. However, both common and civil law systems use variations on the jury concept to supplement the work of judges.

HOW NON-JUDICIAL COURT PERSONNEL SUPPORT ADJUDICATORS

Regardless of legal system or court type, non-judicial personnel perform a variety of functions that support adjudicators and ensure a professional, timely adjudication process. They can also implement techniques to improve the selection, orientation, and use of participants in the adjudication process.

Variations on jurors. In Germany, Macedonia, and some other former communist states, lay judges with no legal qualifications preside with court judges to assist in determining questions of fact. This contrasts with the common law role of a jury, which is to act separately and exclusively from the judge. Lay judges are often appointed for fixed terms (such as two to four years). They sit on the bench next to the judge and have an advantage over jurors because they gain experience over time instead of serving for just

---

[III]Administration includes the supervision of judges and ultimate control over the court's finances, systems, and personnel. In larger and/or modernized courts, non-judicial personnel perform some of these functions.

one trial. In many common law and civil law courts, experts and assessors may assist judges in evaluating technical evidence. Lay judges, experts, assessors, and a variety of personnel with comparable positions in different systems have a role that is jury-like because they participate directly with the judge in determining questions of fact, but not issues of law or procedure.

4. JUDICIAL INDEPENDENCE
Separation of powers principle.

Courts, and therefore judges, are expected to resolve disputes impartially by applying the law without undue influence from the other branches of government. This principle springs from the model of political power called the separation of powers doctrine. This doctrine provides for the formal separation of the legislature, the executive, and the judiciary. Separation is maintained by a system of checks and balances that prevent one branch from dominating either of the other two. Common law systems often view judicial power as quite distinct from executive power. In contrast, many civil law systems view the role of adjudicating as essentially an extension of the role of government rather than a potential counterpoint to it. In both civil and common law systems, judicial independence requires some creative arrangements. This is because courts receive their funding from the legislative branch and judges may have been appointed by the executive branch. However, the perception and maintenance of independence is essential for public support for courts and confidence in the rule of law.

Defining judicial power. Systems that formally separate the judiciary from the executive usually have a large body of codified or case law that defines judicial power. The underlying assumption is that having an institutionally independent judiciary distinct from the executive and the legislature requires enforceable constraints and protections that expressly limit interference by the legislature and the executive in the judiciary's work.

HOW NON-JUDICIAL COURT PERSONNEL SUPPORT JUDICIAL INDEPENDENCE

Court personnel promote judicial independence through competent budget and finance controls, and by fostering strong public relations and transparency in court proceedings. If the judicial system cannot manage its funds, keep control over its own rules and internal discipline, and maintain policies that prevent patronage, it is open to outside influence and attacks on independence. Further, by ensuring accountability for the judiciary and facilitating efficient justice, court personnel can support independence from the other branches. They can also promote innovation to improve services to the public and therefore raise the stature of the court in the public eye.

CHAPTER SUMMARY

The nature of a country's legal system affects how courts operate, the roles of judges, and the interactions of judges with other court personnel. However, irrespective of the classification of a legal system or the procedural traditions of courts, all courts share core common needs:

- The need for an appeals process that can evaluate lower court decisions

- The need for transparent, effective, and publicly accessible court hearings, preferably with a significant oral component

- The need for consistency in decision making

- The need to define and adequately support those who participate directly in the adjudication process, including judges and juries

- The need for judicial independence and the separation of powers

Capable court personnel are vital to meet these needs.

III.MANAGING COURT PERSONNEL

At its most basic, a court can consist of a judge in a temporary or permanent courtroom. The skills and traditions of judging, seasoned by experience with the law, make this simple arrangement effective. However, when a court grows to comprise multiple judges sitting in multiple courtrooms supported by extensive staff, many more management skills are needed. This is especially true at higher levels of the appellate chain where geographic coverage increases.

This chapter describes the structures and practices that influence the management of courts and their personnel on both national and local levels. It presents two models for national-level management of court systems and three models for managing individual courts.

Creating regional arrangements for sharing best practice information and bridging the management gap between the national and local levels is also beneficial. A good example of such co-operation is the use of regional judicial councils and regional managers with specifically defined responsibilities for management and administration.

A. NATIONAL STRUCTURES FOR MANAGING COURTS AND THEIR PERSONNEL[IV]

1. MODELS

There are two basic models for national management of court budgets, resources, and staff:

(1)   The Justice Ministry Model, in which the executive branch, frequently a Ministry of Justice, controls the administrative and budgetary functions

(2)   The Separate Branch Model, in which the judiciary self-governs and exercises budgetary control over judicial system operations through judiciary-based mechanisms, such as a judicial council and the related administrative offices of the courts or court administrators

The Justice Ministry Model. This model, shown in Figure 3, is predominant in Europe. Some reform experts, particularly those with a common law perspective, view this model as less desirable than the separate branch model from the standpoint of judicial independence because it can lead to interference in judicial affairs and to bureaucratic delays. However, it appears to work in countries that are more developed; have democratic, market-based economies; and have a

Figure 3. Justice Ministry Model of Judicial Management

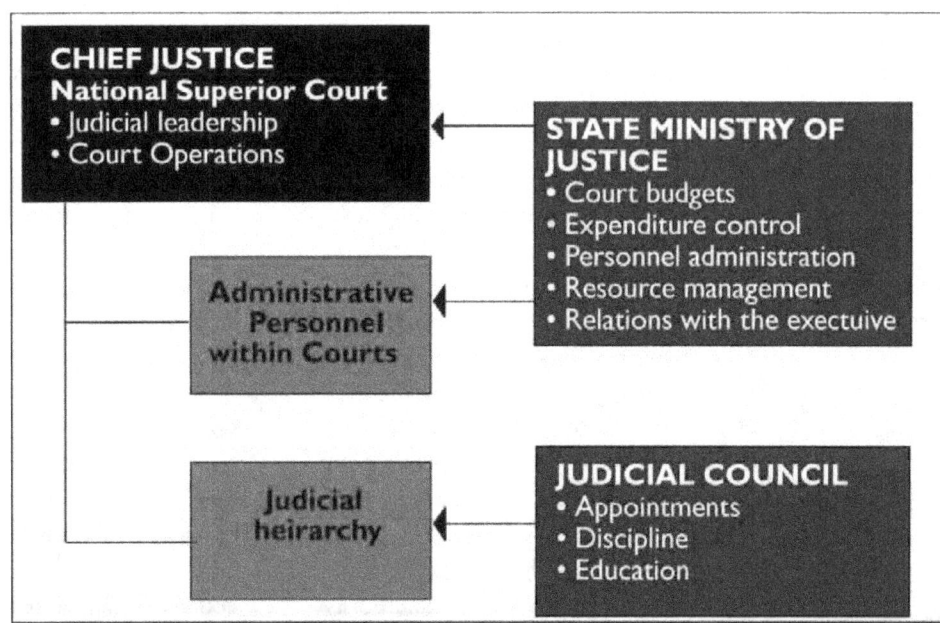

[IV]In some countries, states or other subdivisions may also have macro-level structures for managing courts in their jurisdiction. The models and issues discussed in this section apply to those structures as well.

GUIDE TO COURT REFORM AND THE ROLE OF COURT PERSONNEL - 9

Figure 4. Separate Branch Model of Judicial Management

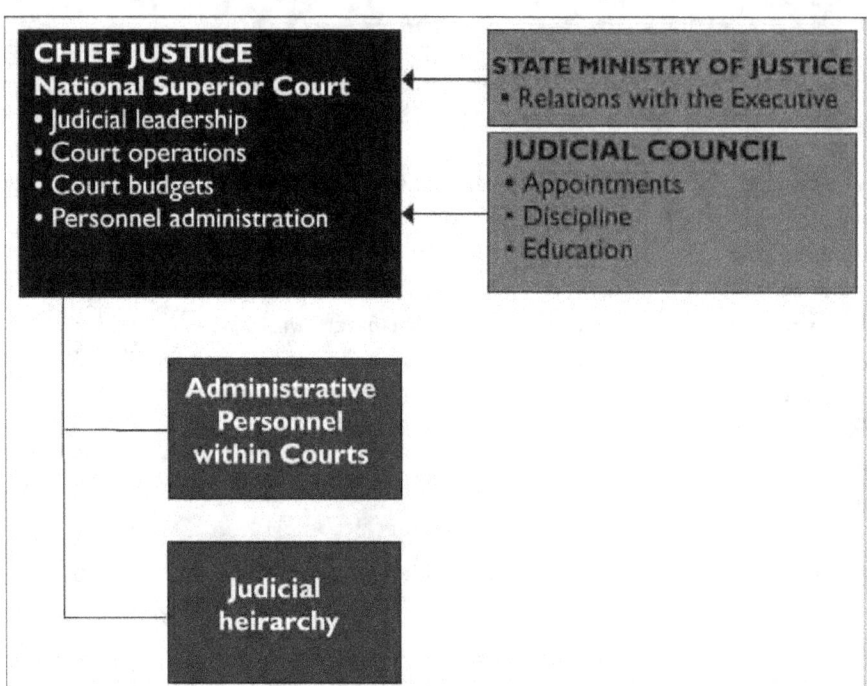

traditionally stable and responsible executive government. In countries that are unstable, autocratic, or vulnerable to institutional corruption, this model can significantly compromise judicial independence and, consequentially, the effectiveness of courts.

The Separate Branch Model. This model, shown in Figure 4, is based on self-government or independent administration of budgets, personnel, and other organizational functions. With budgetary and resource autonomy, the judicial system has substantial and final influence over the size of the judicial budget and the priorities to which it is allocated. Under this model, the Ministry of Justice, or equivalent body, has only a subordinate role.

2. REFORM ISSUES AND ALTERNATIVES

Governance issues. A key issue in court personnel and management reform is whether the judicial system has a governance or management framework for overseeing and supporting individual courts. To be effective, the

judicial system needs the capacity to carry out central budget and policy-making authority. The governance methods outlined below are not mutually exclusive and can be used in combination.

Judicial councils. One avenue for administrative reform is the delegation of administrative oversight to judicial councils. Many countries, especially those with civil law systems, have established judicial councils or commissions with powers ranging from the appointment and discipline of judges to the administration of courts and judiciaries. These councils may be established under a national constitution or by legislation. They often have non-judicial members, such as government ministers, legislators, chief prosecutors, or legal profession representatives. Where a council is solely concerned with recommending judicial appointments, it has a minimal impact on the managerial structures of courts. However, in some systems, judicial councils have broad policy-making authority over the court system and can substi-

tute for a justice minister or even a chief justice in administrative management of the courts. Judicial councils can also supervise court administrative offices.

Administrative offices of the court. Administrative offices, which provide centralized service and support to all court personnel, operate under the direction of the chief justice and, where one exists, the judicial council. The administrative office provides guidance, monitoring, and support for the administrative areas that are vital for court operations. Typical duties are (1) preparing and administering the judicial budget, (2) paying all court salaries and expenses, (3) managing property and facilities, (4) statistical reporting of court data, (5) distributing supplies and equipment for the courts, (6) supporting information technology, (7) jury administration, (8) communicating with relevant government offices, and (9) directing educational programs for court staff. Where there is a judicial council, the administrative office implements council policies.

Professional court administrators.
The appointment of a chief of court administration permits a court system to reinforce its administrative independence by reliance on a chief executive whose first loyalty is to the judiciary rather than to the executive. This concept of a professional court administrator has proven effective in U.S., Western European, and many developing country court systems.

FACILITATING TRANSFER

If administrative control is transferred to a judicial or independent entity without first, or simultaneously, establishing the capability of judicial or administrative leaders to carry out their responsibilities effectively, all of the courts will suffer. For example, lack of professional court management in Spain's Basque region resulted in the transfer of administrative control back to the ministry of justice.[*] In contrast, when the Hungarian government transferred administrative authority to the judicial system in the late 1980s, the government ensured that the judicial system quickly developed the necessary competence by transferring to the judiciary a number of experts previously employed by the Ministry of Justice. These personnel provided the new Administrative Bureau of the Judicial Council with the expertise and professional credibility it needed and eliminated the delays that would have resulted from recruiting, hiring, and training a cadre of new budgetary and administrative experts.

USAID Guide for Promoting Judicial Independence and Impartiality, January 2002.

Pursuing self-management. Rule of law programs often advocate for constitutional and legislative changes that reform the relationship between the executive and the judiciary. The explicit aims are to make the judiciary more independent and to give it more managerial autonomy. However, in some systems, both executive and judicial branches are resistant to this kind of reform for historical and political reasons. This makes it hard to decide how to remedy institutional or structural features that prevent courts from achieving the independence essential for managing their own resources and personnel. One option is to improve the capacity for self-management, to the extent that it is permitted. Courts that are internally well managed can often increase their ability both to influence the budgetary process and to ensure that court expenditures reflect the needs of the court. Similarly, more effective self-management can enable the courts to use personnel to meet court needs, rather than to meet objectives or perform tasks defined by actors outside the judicial system.

Limitations on reforming administration. Under any model, the power to appoint and employ court personnel may be sharply constrained by government regulation, thereby limiting the extent to which the judiciary can use personnel and budgetary resources to meet court needs. The formal relationship between the executive, the judiciary, and the various institutional elements that may be established for governing the judiciary can often obscure the true source of control over judicial management. Further, there may be a willingness to transfer administrative but not budgetary control, or only to share budget control. Such partial administrative autonomy may lead to a conflict-prone judicial management process. Also, establishing mechanisms for control of the courts is not the same as establishing well-managed courts. For example, a disagreement between a justice minister and a chief justice about who should control a court budget is irrelevant if neither the ministry nor the judiciary can manage funds without corruption or misuse. Consequently, an important priority for a court system is the adequacy of its internal structures and governance. If the transition of administrative authority is not carried out properly, the judicial system will not reap the benefits of independence or efficiency.

B. INDIVIDUAL COURT MANAGEMENT

This section describes three models for individual court management: (1) judges as court administrators, (2) judicial cadre management, where several judges head different functional units, and (3) professional court management by non-judicial personnel.

1. JUDGES AS COURT ADMINISTRATORS

The traditional court manager is a chief judge[v] who directs the daily operations of the court in addition to judging. These tasks could include creating the roster of judges, allocating cases, and overseeing all staff and their functions. However, as courts grow in size and complexity, the burden on judges administering courts often results in organizational mismanagement and misuse of judicial talent.

a. MANAGEMENT MODELS
This section illustrates variations in the judicial management approach and the function of non-judicial staff in judge-managed courts.

Chief judges. At the top of a typical court structure is a chief judge who is empowered to represent and administer the court. Irrespective of court size, the chief judge generally is an active judge, often presiding at the head of the

---

[v]Some systems use different titles, such as senior judge or court president.

most important cases that come before the court. The chief judge also serves as institutional figurehead, responsible for managing the court's administration and relationships with other institutions. A chief judge usually has more non-judicial staff than a judge without administrative responsibilities. A chief judge may also seek the assistance of deputy-level judges in general court administration.

MISUSE OF JUDICIAL TALENT

In one Middle Eastern country, each business day the chief judge of a large urban court personally signs hundreds of criminal background record check certificates prepared by court staff because the signature authority cannot be delegated.

In a large urban trial court in Central Europe, the chief judge must personally manage the fleet of court vehicles and personally oversee repairs and renovations to court facilities.

In both cases, the chief judges are highly experienced judges with considerable expertise. They may successfully juggle both judicial and administrative responsibilities, but this arrangement diminishes the efficiency of court operations.

Collegial governance. In career judiciaries, typical of civil law systems where judges enter the profession immediately after law school, the relationships between judges of different courts may be hierarchical. However, the chief judges of most courts manage collegially, at least when they are based in the same location, referring major administrative decisions to committees of judges or plenary meetings of judges before deciding them. The same is true of court units, such as criminal judges or family court judges, in larger courts. When decisions affecting judges need to be made, all the judges expect that

they will be consulted and that decisions will be reached only with majority or unanimous support. Thus, the chief judge tends to act as a first among equals.

In some systems, the collegial approach is reinforced by the short tenure of the chief judge, who may be appointed based strictly on seniority. Judges who are automatically promoted to these positions may reach retirement age soon thereafter, to be replaced by the next-most-senior judge. Consequently, some courts rely on committees of judges to make essential organizational decisions, as this process assures continuity between regularly changing leaders.

Judge administrators. Judge administrator positions may be formally established in some courts or may develop as a casual delegation of responsibility. Like a chief judge, a judge administrator continues in his or her adjudicatory role, but also spends time on administrative supervision. The judge administrator's work may be limited to traditionally judicial tasks (such as case allocation to other judges or active supervision of docket management across a group of judges) or to the supervision of a division of non-judicial personnel within the court administration (such as a central registry or process serving office). Judge administrators relieve chief judges of the burden of court administration and help support the work of judicial committees that may be used to sustain collegial governance systems in large courts. They are also especially useful in courts that lack a professional cadre of non-judicial personnel.

Non-judicial court personnel support for judge managers. In relatively small, simple courts, non-judicial personnel are generally secretarial and administrative staff attached to a particular judge. As employees of an insti-

tution that in many countries is part of a government ministry, these personnel are usually hired under civil service rules. In some instances, however, the personal staff of judges may be employed under arrangements that give judges broad discretion to select staff and terminate their employment at will. These practices can lead to the perceived or real problems of nepotism and cronyism. Courts in all systems should organize and regulate the employment of non-judicial personnel in a fair and economical manner.

b. SUPPORT STAFF SERVING INDIVIDUAL JUDGES

Judge-focused support staff. In some courts, the personnel structure provides for staff who serve an individual judge. This structure is called judge-focused. Illustrated in Figure 5, it contrasts with the option of arranging some court staff into functional divisions that perform tasks centrally on behalf of all judges. Under this structure, employees may perform most of the functions for a judge, while proportionally few staff members are dedicated to administering centralized common services, such as salaries processing or records archive management.

INEFFICIENCIES OF THE JUDGE-FOCUSED STAFF MODEL

In some countries of the Indian subcontinent, the personal staff of each judge often performs a full range of services, including all aspects of case management from filing to enforcement. The staff effectively provides a self-contained court registry for each judge within a court. As a result, those courts often lack central registries or any form of general court administration staff. Thus, they are significantly overstaffed with poorly paid and under-skilled non-judicial personnel who do not implement best practices.

Figure 5. Judge-Focused Support Staff

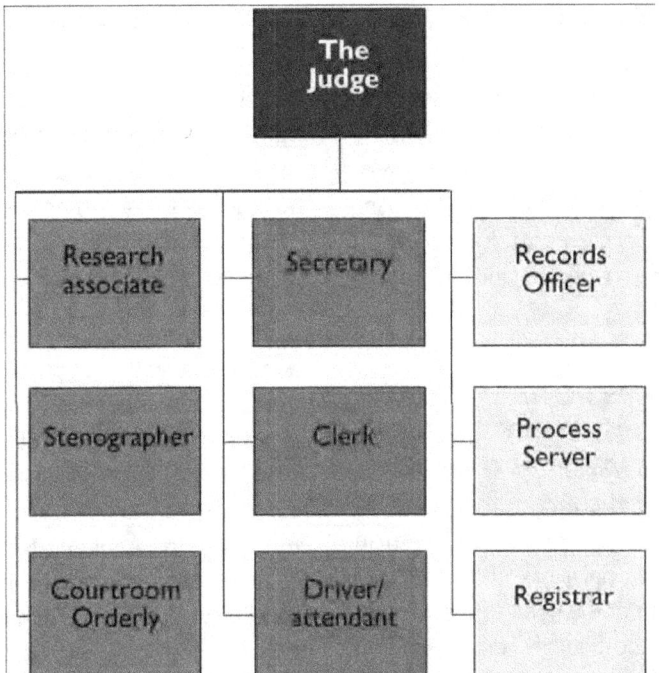

Limited utility of judge-focused staff. Depending on the range of staff competencies, this model can serve the needs of an individual judge, who manages and supervises the staff. However, in terms of meeting the court's broader organizational needs, this arrangement is less satisfactory and more costly. There is no economy of scale or division of labor in processing the work of the court as a whole (for example, a pool of clerks or secretaries); the staff may be incapable of carrying out all of the necessary tasks; and there may be redundant personnel and supervision. A court that operates on a small scale can work best with judge-focused staff, but when workloads are high or complex, as in large urban courts, this model for organizing non-judicial per-

sonnel offers considerably less capacity and flexibility to respond effectively.

Moreover, the capacity of judges to exercise effective authority over their staff depends on the judges' managerial skills. Judges in most court systems typically come not from civil service ranks but from the executive branch, private bar, academia, or law schools. Few have the experience or capacity for staff supervision. Thus, the development of effective court staff organizations is often limited to a judge's ability to influence the selection and management of his or her own personal staff.

While the judge-focused staff system is perhaps the least efficient way to structure court personnel, efforts to reform these systems are frequently resisted by the staff themselves, who are often very loyal to "their" judge and are unwilling to accept reassignment.

2. JUDICIAL CADRE MANAGEMENT

Multiple judges as managers. Court organizations that delegate administration roles to judges rather than to non-judicial personnel use a judicial cadre management system. Under this system, judges head and manage judicial staff units or functional branches staffed by non-judicial personnel (Figure 6).

Both civil and common law systems have been slow to recognize the value of developing senior non-judicial court administrators. One likely reason is that the evolution of modern courts has been influenced primarily by the imperative to achieve judicial independence. In many systems, this goal has been taken to mean that judges assume more responsibility and administrators less. In some systems, reliance on judicial cadres is high and is viewed as a means to protect a judiciary from interference; reinforce the choices and prerogatives of judges; and provide quality control in administration, which in some countries can be difficult to gain

Figure 6. Judicial Cadre Management System

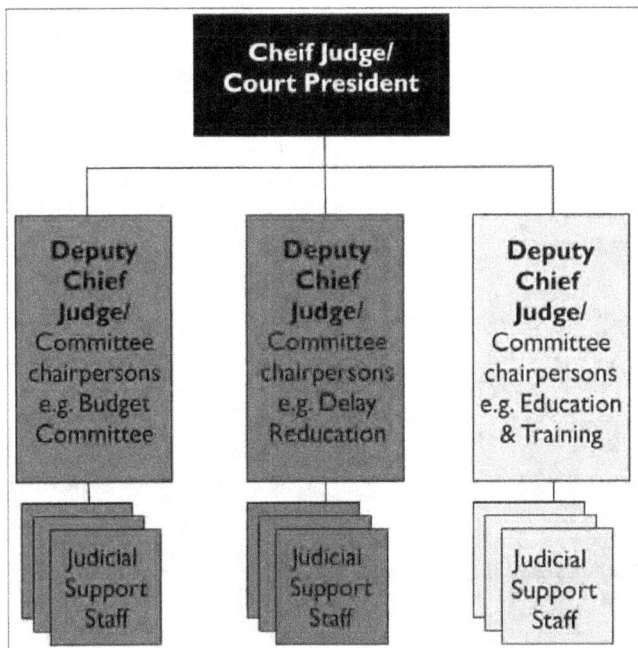

from non-judicial court personnel. Consequently, reforms in some courts have entailed judges loyal to the court gradually asserting greater control over court administration in lieu of bureaucrats who were often more likely to be loyal to the executive branch.

Delegation to non-judicial court staff. In some courts, administrative roles are delegated not only to judges, but also to non-judicial staff, such as court secretaries, registrars, court clerks, or other similar officers. A court secretary, for example, is a non-judicial officer who holds a senior administrative position in a court and may or may not have university law qualifications. A registrar is generally an administrator who has university law qualifications and who might exercise quasi-judicial functions, such as presiding at administrative and procedural hearings. Non-judicial staff can also manage the important uncontested civil work of a court.

Positions such as these are often suited to the needs of judge administrators who preside at small rural or urban courts with few judges, or at courts that move about, such as circuit courts. In effect, establishing non-judicial administrative positions has allowed systems that relied on judicial cadre management approaches to draw in the skilled support of non-judicial court personnel.

3. PROFESSIONAL COURT MANAGEMENT BY NON-JUDICIAL PERSONNEL

Professional court managers. The development of modern caseflow management principles has led to a gradual recognition of the need to train court personnel, both judges and non-judges, to be effective managers. This new philosophy has required courts to introduce new case management processes and has also required all judges to adopt these changes. It has led to the development of workflow systems; information systems; and common processes for issuing documents, scheduling hearings, and managing trials. Judges and non-judicial court personnel frequently lack the knowledge and skills to implement these reforms. Caseflow management requires professional administrators who can work alongside judges to implement the new systems.

Thus, following the U.S. model, professional court administrators now lead the development of modern courts in many civil and common law systems, including courts in the United Kingdom, Canada, Australia, New Zealand, and Singapore. Additionally, some Western European and Latin American courts have introduced administrative reform to coincide with broader public sector management and economic reforms. Introducing new court management systems allows judges and court personnel to work together to improve court efficiency and effectiveness.

A professional court administrator may lead a functional unit of non-judicial staff, each dedicated to a specific organizational objective. Judges continue to lead the court, including committees and all aspects of the adjudication. However, they rely on administrators to inform their work, implement administrative systems, and manage the court. At the top of the administrative hierarchy, a chief administrator answers to the chief judge of the court and operates as the chief judge's executive officer. The chief judge oversees the court as a whole, including both judicial committees and administrative functions and personnel (Figure 7).

Modernizing court personnel management. Success in modernizing court personnel management depends on more than merely introducing new court administrators. It requires a wholesale change in a court's approach to governance. This change

Figure 7. Professional Court Administration

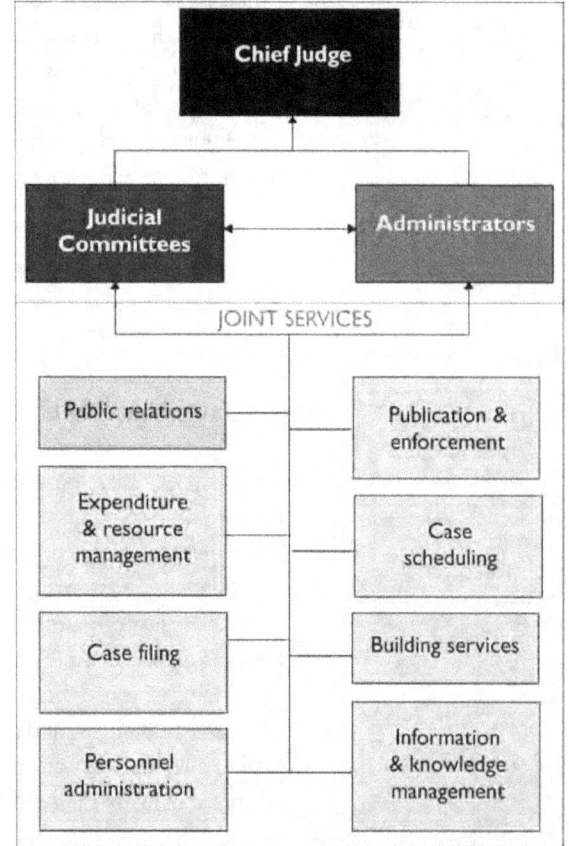

includes redefining accepted notions of judicial leadership, willingness to develop and use organized systems of work, and a commitment to increasing internal and external transparency of those systems.

Basics of modernization. Many countries that have successfully modernized courts and court personnel management have also enjoyed national economic growth, civil and political stability, broad public sector management reforms, and improved access to low-cost technology. Reform may be more difficult in other environments. Nonetheless, the process for court modernization is common to all court systems. It requires all courts to develop and maintain explicit and transparent cost-effective systems for all of their functions. To implement this reform, judges who lead courts need to adopt more sophisticated systems of court management and to delegate the day-to-day administration of those systems to professional court administrators and the other court personnel who assist them.

CHAPTER SUMMARY

Understanding options for national and individual court management structures is important to understanding the roles of court personnel. It is also important to understanding how these personnel can help ensure an efficient and effective judicial system. Well-established management structures are vital for fulfilling judicial needs and for maximizing the use of court personnel. Key reforms include creating judicial councils, administrative offices, and professionalized court administrators. As a judicial system and individual courts become larger and more complex, there are greater needs for:

- Moving away from executive branch–controlled administration

- Centralized court staff as opposed to judge-focused staff

- Professionalized court managers with operational and leadership capacities.

IV. THE USE OF COURT PERSONNEL IN SUPPORTING CORE COURT FUNCTIONS

Designing rule of law programs that target court personnel reform requires understanding what courts do. This provides the foundation for defining the services that court personnel should provide and therefore the types of staff needed. This chapter profiles the core processes of courts, identifies the roles and competencies of court personnel in administering them, and shows how appropriate use of court personnel improves court efficiency and effectiveness. Some court systems have too few personnel. Others have too many, often of the wrong type, not professionalized, or in positions because of patronage. Even where staffing is adequate, courts may suffer from archaic procedural codes or a lack of modern practices and technology. Court personnel and management reforms can address these problems.

A. CORE COURT FUNCTIONS

Case adjudication as a core process. Case adjudication refers to the process by which courts hear and decide a case. The procedure may be oral or documentary. Case adjudication typically culminates in a trial, followed by publication, appeal and review if necessary, and enforcement. Therefore, most of the steps preceding the trial are geared toward preparing the case for trial. Although in many efficient civil and criminal court systems only a mi-

nority of cases goes to trial, the capacity of courts to try cases drives all other types of case disposal. This is because the courts' power to try cases gives them leverage to persuade litigants to consider alternative means of case settlement, such as conciliation, negotiated settlement, and plea bargaining.

Phases of case adjudication. Figure 8 shows nine phases of judicial case adjudication and systems associated with them. These phases represent the core business of courts and typically apply to both civil and criminal cases. The following sub-sections describe each phase, the roles of non-judicial court personnel relevant to each phase, and factors to consider in project de-

Figure 8. Essential Phases and Systems of Case Adjudication

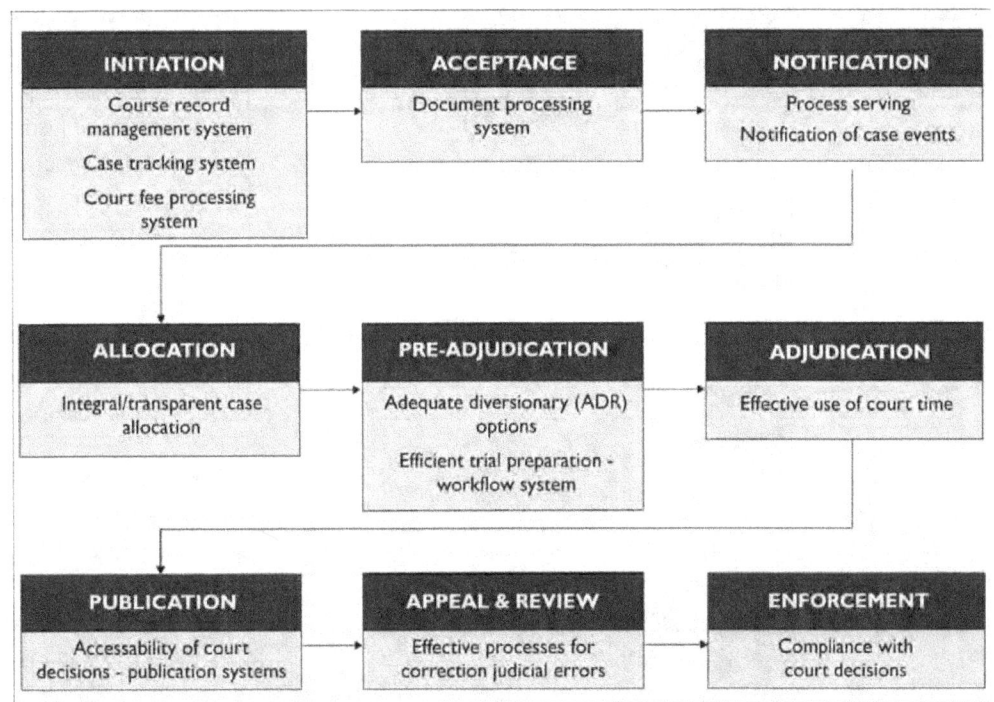

sign. The purpose is to map the use of court personnel in areas that court reform activities often target under rule of law programs.

B. INITIATION – PHASE 1

Case initiation is the event that brings a court to intervene and attempt to resolve a dispute. To support initiation, effectively managed courts have:

- A case register and tracking system

- An accounting system for court fees

- A record management system

- Procedures to prevent corruption

- Trained, supervised personnel to administer case filing

Filing and registration. Most court procedures require recording a summary of the newly filed case in a registry. Most courts use register books, which are large ledger-type books in which the summary of each case is handwritten or typed into a specified entry space. Moreover, most courts use multiple manual registry books to record case information in different formats; frequently, the same information is entered several times. This makes preparing and maintaining manual register books very labor-intensive. Therefore, modern court systems increasingly substitute computerized case tracking systems for register books. Cutting-edge courts are introducing electronic filing, and are making those files accessible to the bar and sometimes to the public via the Internet. By eliminating most paper documents,

such systems dramatically improve judicial and non-judicial staff productivity.

FIGHTING CORRUPTION

To combat corruption in Ecuador, windows were placed in the case filing area to allow the public to see the work of the registrars or clerks and ensure that case filing and assignment processes were transparent. Physically separating the staff from the public by windows and slots prevented the parties from having direct access to the court staff, thus reducing opportunities for bribery.

Filing fees. Except for criminal proceedings, most courts impose a filing fee. Court fees are legitimate user charges to help support the court's work and offset its costs. However, fees should not be so high that they prevent access to courts for resolution of serious litigation. Court rules and regulations set the amount of the fee and may also permit fees to be waived or refunded. The collection of filing fees requires procedures that ensure proper accounting of fees collected, prevent corruption, and make the granting of fee waivers transparent.

PROBLEMS WITH FILING

In Afghanistan, most courts require claims to be filed initially with the Afghan Ministry of Justice. The ministry is responsible for processing case records and arranging service of claims on all parties before sending the file to the court. With degraded public services in Afghanistan, this practice results in postponing the court's role, often for years, while it waits to receive the case file from the ministry.

Court records systems. Courts need a system for publicly recording each court action (Figure 9), beginning with filing. The case filing process must be transparent, in terms of where the filing takes place and what the docu-

Figure 9. Elements of Court Records Systems

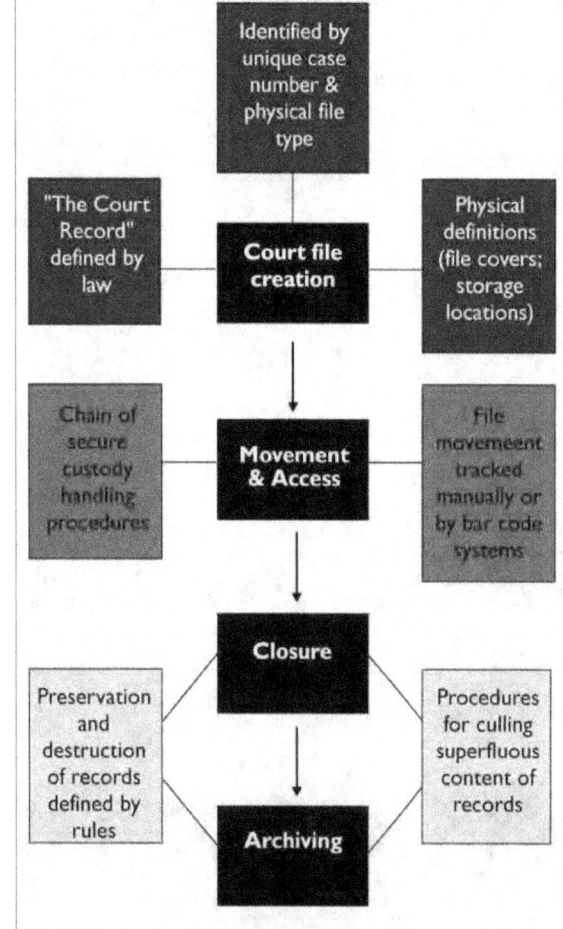

ments contain. Courts can assure transparency by using a clear filing procedure that allows the litigants to access the case initiation document or complaint. That document, known generally as the court record or case file, is maintained as a public record.

The phenomenon of "lost" or misplaced court records is an example of corrupt practices by court staff. As long as the court record or a key element of it is inaccessible, the court cannot act and justice is delayed. Thus, at the time of case filing, courts must ensure that (1) the court record for the case is

created, (2) the case receives an identifying number, (3) the initiating process goes into the record, and (4) the record is securely stored in a place that is under continuous court control.

Non-judicial court personnel in case initiation. Cases are generally filed in the registry or intake office, where court staff receive, examine, and file-stamp documents. The registry or intake personnel include reception staff, intake clerks, examining officers, couriers, accounting officers, and supervisors. These personnel ensure the secure receipt and processing of new files and accountability for fees paid or waived.

C. ACCEPTANCE – PHASE 2

In this phase, the court accepts the case. Effectively managed courts:

- Have a document management system to track the checking and acceptance or rejection of the case

- Defer formal acceptance of a case until the court determines whether it has jurisdiction

- Minimize reliance on non-judicial personnel to check and approve filing documents that initiate process

Initiating service of process. To initiate service of process, a claimant or prosecutor must ensure that filings comply with court standards. Typical filing document standards include the following: (1) compliance with the prescribed format; (2) adequate identification of the parties to the dispute; and (3) sufficient information to satisfy the court that it has jurisdiction to hear and determine the case. The respondent has to accept and respond to the initiating document, and the response filed must also conform to certain standards. Effectively managed courts ad-

minister this process through a document management system that tracks and documents service of process and all other documents filed later.

Document checking. All courts have a system to review case initiation documents (and those subsequently filed) for conformity with established rules. The rigor of the review process can vary widely. Some courts employ strict review standards. In courts where tolerances of error are more generous or where there are good lines of communication between the court and the filing party, errors or defects in initiating documents can be readily overcome. In some systems, documents are accepted on the condition that they may be rejected later if found to be defective. Alternatively, documents may be accepted on the condition that if defects that are not serious are found later, the filing party agrees to correct them promptly.

In high-volume courts that have developed bureaucratic systems, specialized checking officers may formally inspect each document filed. These systems are devoted to the process of identifying defects at or after filing, and issuing requests for corrective action requiring the filing party to amend and re-initiate the filing, sometimes paying additional fees. Stringent document checking is costly. Modern court systems seek to minimize the investment of time and labor by ensuring that the process is clearly defined; that the filing standards are widely available; and that, for those who need them, self-help packets are available to guide unrepresented litigants through the process of preparing and submitting case documents. The idea is to get the document right the first time.

Streamlining acceptance processes. Some courts have streamlined systems for document filing, rejecting only those that lack a critical piece of information, such as the correct name of the filing party. Electronic filing systems facilitate these innovations. They avoid the labor costs associated with meticulous review, either because the prospect of a significant error is low or because the cost of rectifying it later is not high. This reform has simplified standards checking to a point where only fundamental defects are grounds for rejection at the time of filing.

Judicial admission of new cases. In some court systems, the acceptance of initiating civil process is not complete upon filing, even after checking. These systems require acceptance of the initiating process by a judge as a formal judicial act. This requirement reflects traditional rules of practice specifying that courts should not require a person to answer a claim unless first satisfied that there is a case to answer. In some systems acceptance occurs when the case is first assigned to a judge. Like stringent document checking, judicial admission makes case acceptance relatively costly.

Non-judicial court personnel in case acceptance. Some courts maintain separate divisions of clerical and administrative personnel to check and approve initiating process. These personnel may be registrars or senior clerks with experience and detailed knowledge of court rules. Courts that use streamlined processes require less skilled acceptance staff. Registry staff alone can administer both filing and acceptance processes at the time of

---

FACTORS TO CONSIDER IN PROJECT DESIGN

Is there a transparent system for checking the initiating process?

Is there a formal judicial admission process for new cases? If so, is it minimized to assure effective use of judicial time?

---

filing. Well-designed filing systems have built-in check points that require the filing party to ensure that the filing conforms to the required standards. When these systems are in place, court personnel assume the role of quality control specialists who review the filed documents to ensure their compliance.

D. NOTIFICATION – PHASE 3

This phase includes notification of the parties and scheduling the case. Effectively managed courts have:

- A document production system enabling the court to produce and deliver notices to the parties

- A court bailiff system that enables courts to serve initiating documents on parties independently by direct delivery or other practical means

- A court hearing scheduling system that enables effective scheduling of case dates

Service of initiating process or summons. Notifying all parties to a civil suit or criminal prosecution is a core prerequisite of case adjudication. The purposes of a summons are to provide information and to require the defendant to respond.

Preparing a summons. Some courts have only manual systems for processing new cases. Most of these courts require the plaintiff or prosecutor to file multiple copies of the initiating process so that the additional copies may be served on the other parties. Courts with automated document production systems often prefer to issue their own documents for delivery, particularly when these documents are produced using court computer databases.

Non-judicial court personnel in case notification. In courts that merely stamp multiple copies of accepted initiating process, registry clerks who process case filings often perform case notification. Other courts must produce new documents in response to a filing. In non-automated courts, typists often perform this task. Some automated courts use computerized case register and tracking systems that can produce documents, requiring court personnel with the necessary computer and organizational skills.

Scheduling. Most courts have rules for scheduling the first hearing date. These rules should be transparent and consistently applied.

Non-judicial court personnel in scheduling. Although judges may directly allocate dates for cases in their dockets, ordinarily a court registry official or clerk sets the first hearing date for a case according to the rules. The court staff must be well-supervised to avoid corrupt practices, such as selling opportunities to expedite or delay a case's first hearing date. Their duties should include maintaining a case hearing diary to record all initial case hearings, and maintaining, producing, and distributing daily calendars of all hearings scheduled before each judge.

Non-judicial court personnel in process serving. Courts may have a bailiff or similar officer to serve process. A bailiff may be attached either to the court or to an associated government agency. In some court systems, process serving may be contracted out to a court-approved or licensed private process server. In some civil law systems, the police serve process. Other court personnel can also be used to serve court process. Courts with appropriate resources and technology can use postal service and electronic delivery, such as facsimile or e-mail, as a substitute for in-person process serving. In those cases, registry clerks may be used in lieu of bailiffs, often using computerized document production systems.

Other methods of process serving. More advanced court systems, particularly in the U.S., have shifted a major portion of the responsibility for service of process from the courts to the litigants. For example, when a civil complaint is filed with the court, the filing party rather than the court is responsible for serving a copy of the complaint on the respondent and for issuing a certificate of service of process that is filed with the court. When the respondent files an answer to the complaint with the court, he or she also is required to serve the plaintiff with a copy of the response. This procedure relieves the courts of a significant burden. In well-designed electronic filing systems, the filing party serves copies on the court and on the other parties to the dispute electronically rather than in a hardcopy format.

FACTORS TO CONSIDER IN PROJECT DESIGN

Who is responsible for notifying defendants and respondents?

Does the court use bailiffs or rely on outside resources for process serving?

Is there a system for scheduling hearings? Are the personnel competent to ensure that the hearing schedule is effectively managed and free from corruption?

E. ALLOCATION – PHASE 4

This phase involves assigning cases to judges. Effectively managed courts have transparent case assignment systems that are formula-based or random, thus minimizing or eliminating discretion.

Referring cases to judges. When a court has only one judge, there is no

question as to who will receive the case. Larger courts with more than one judge require a process to assign cases in a manner that promotes transparency, minimizes manipulation, and precludes "judge shopping" by the parties. Poorly designed assignment systems may facilitate corruption or unfair practices. If the case allocation process is informal and controlled by unsupervised staff, a party may exert undue influence to have the case assigned to a more sympathetic, less impartial, or unethical judge.

Allocation systems. There are four types of allocation systems: (1) discretionary, (2) formula-based, (3) automated random, and (4) mixed. Most court systems in developing countries use a combination of the first three, resulting in a mixed method system.

Discretionary allocation. Many court systems across the world give discretion to a chief judge (or another senior judge) to allocate cases. The chief judge reviews newly initiated cases and decides to whom each case will be assigned. The allocation is often based on the need to balance the judicial workload. This involves reviewing the workload of each judge and assigning new cases to the judges whose workloads appear lightest. The chief judge receives case records or a list of new cases and assigns each case, making allowance for those that require special or urgent attention. However, such an allocation system can incorporate a degree of formula-based sorting to make the process less onerous and more predictable. For example, the lists may be pre-sorted by court personnel and marked for allocation according to a formula. The chief judge has discretion to override this formula for complex or difficult cases as long as the procedure is transparent and properly documented.

Formula-based allocation. Formula-based assignment systems function automatically without discretionary judgment. One such system allocates each new case on a revolving basis to the next judge scheduled to receive a case according to a mathematical formula. In the Philippines, some trial courts employ a system of case lotteries to ensure that judges have a say in deciding which cases are allocated to them. Such systems can produce unsatisfactory imbalances of workload among judges, but they are rational, transparent, consistent, and less vulnerable to corruption. They can also be very efficient because they are not dependent on a high level of supervision or discretionary control.

FORMULA-BASED CASE ALLOCATION

Using a formula-based allocation system enables courts to eliminate the human factor in the case assignment process. In the lower courts in Delhi, India, minor offense cases are allocated to judges based on which police station prosecutes the charge. In a large, multi-judge court, each judge is responsible for cases originating from a designated group of police stations. The charges are filed directly in the courtrooms of the designated judges with no involvement by either the senior judge or a court registry.

Automated random assignment. Some court systems, such as the Slovak courts and the U.S. federal trial and appellate courts, assign cases using automated random assignment protocols. These systems have the benefits of no human intervention and a random process that defies efforts to anticipate to whom the next case will be assigned. Typically, these systems are designed and maintained by court information technology staff under the supervision of the court administrator and chief judge.

Mixed allocation methods. In some high-volume courts that may have only modest imbalances in the workload, such as traffic courts, the cases may be allocated mechanically by a numerically balanced random assignment, as if dealing a deck of cards. The process is more complicated where the judges differ in their areas of specialization, experience, and/or facility in processing their workload. Under these conditions, the assignment may also have a discretionary component, with the chief judge taking into account (1) the type and complexity of the case, (2) the differing competencies and specializations of the available judges, and (3) the case's impact on the workload of the assigned judge. In courts that have large backlogs and case delays, these considerations become more difficult to apply.

MISALLOCATION OF CASES
Some African courts use a purposeful assignment system that assigns cases to certain judges with more experience or knowledge, but this system poses risks of improper influence or corruption. For example, in Kenya, the chief justice assigned constitutional cases and certain civil disputes to particular judges, and the duty judge assigned all other cases. Duty judges tended to allocate to themselves any remaining politically sensitive cases and then proceeded to dismiss them, preventing justice from being served.[*]

USAID Guide for Promoting Judicial Independence and Impartiality, January 2002.

Prevention of corruption and unfair influence. Formula-based or random allocation systems prevent corruption. Formula-based systems require taking due care to ensure that parties do not learn how to manipulate the formula. In the absence of formula-based or random allocation systems,

the most senior and, hopefully, most impartial judge available should make the discretionary decision on case allocation.

Non-judicial court personnel in case allocation. Except where computer systems handle case allocation, most courts designate certain staff to assist in administering case assignment systems. These may be personal staff of the relevant senior judge. In court systems that can implement formula-based allocation systems, registry officials who are involved in case filing and acceptance processing also do the allocation.

FACTORS TO CONSIDER IN PROJECT DESIGN

Are case allocation systems formula-based, random, or discretionary?

How does the system ensure integrity and transparency?

Can judicial or non-judicial personnel make subsequent changes that subvert the integrity of initial case allocation?

F. PRE-ADJUDICATION – PHASE 5

This phase includes pre-trial processes, including facilitating readiness for trail and scheduling. Effectively managed courts use and enforce case preparation schedules.

Systems for case preparation. The combined pressures exerted by large caseloads, backlogs, and poorly motivated or undisciplined litigants can result in inefficient use of the court's time during the pre-trial phase. They can also increase the elapsed time between significant events. Most backlogged cases are in the pre-trial phase as a result of failures on the part of at least one party. A court's ability to prevent these failures depends on enforcing realistic case preparation timetables, in

addition to encouraging settlement and negotiation.

Caseflow management principles emphasize the importance of courts offering litigants firm and credible trial dates as an incentive to settle or to limit the scope of their disputes. Consequently, one measure of success in introducing these principles is a reduction in the number of times that case proceedings are adjourned or continued.

Facilitating readiness for trial. Court efforts in the pre-trial stage focus on (1) facilitating the exchange of evidence and related information among the parties; (2) narrowing the legal issues; (3) establishing a schedule of all critical dates, including a firm trial date; (4) identifying which witnesses will be heard; and (5) determining whether the dispute can be resolved by alternatives to the formal trial process.

Keeping to the schedule. To keep to the established schedule (see example in Figure 10), the judge must manage the case firmly and objectively, establishing clear expectations early, and affirming to the parties that the schedule will be not be modified barring some emergency and a showing of good cause. If the judge cedes management of scheduling to the parties, deadlines will likely not be met. Ineffective judges routinely grant continuances or extensions without requiring parties to show good cause. Also, when scheduling case proceedings, ineffective judges routinely schedule hearings to handle only a single pre-trial or trial issue, resulting in a scheduling sequence strung out over an extended period. In contrast, effective judges typically schedule the final pre-trial and trial stages of adjudication in one extended proceeding.

Non-judicial court personnel in monitoring the schedule. Court staff assist judges in monitoring the status of cases assigned to them. When

Figure 10. A Sample Civil Case Preparation Schedule

(based on court approval of the schedule on 1 February)

1. All parties may initiate the issue of subpoenas to third parties for production of documents to the court within 30 days of issue; all parties may inspect documents produced under subpoena.	**Subpoenas to issue by 15 March**
2. All parties attend a court-annexed mediation conference.	**1 March**
3. Plaintiff files and serves particulars of claim with affidavits in support.	**15 March**
4. Defendant files and serves its response with affidavits in support.	**30 March**
5. Each party files and serves a list of documents on which it intends to rely.	**15 April**
6. Each party enables inspection of its documents by other parties.	**20 to 30 April**
7. Final pre-trial conference establishes time required for trial.	**1 May**
8. Trial commences for three weeks.	**1 July**

a particular case requires judicial attention, they schedule a status conference. Where a court-imposed deadline for a submission has passed, they contact the party to provide a reminder.

FACTORS TO CONSIDER IN PROJECT DESIGN

Does the court demand and enforce adequate trial preparation by the parties?

Does the court enforce an adjournment policy to assure compliance with its approved schedules?

Are the trial dates allocated by the court firm?

G. ADJUDICATION – PHASE 6

Figure 11 illustrates the main stages of a trial for most courts across the world. Effectively managed courts have:

- Oral hearing management systems for accurate recording, evidence presentation, and evidence management

- Adequate and well-trained courtroom staff and resources to assure the effectiveness of oral hearings

Continuous vs. serial trials. Wherever possible, effectively managed courts in both common law and civil law systems conduct trials continuously or near continuously. A continuous trial means that a judge or a judicial panel conducts the trial in a particular case from start to closing submissions and with minimal interruptions. However, some courts break the trial into several discrete components. Under a serial hearing system, each stage may be scheduled for at least one separate hearing. Sometimes each can require a number of hearings. This can cut costs by deciding issues that are likely to determine the case early or shorten the duration of later hearings.

Oral hearing management. The purpose of a courtroom hearing is to permit a judge (and jury when present) to view and hear evidence of witnesses and submissions by legal representatives. Many courtroom system innova-

Figure 11. The Main Stages of a Trial

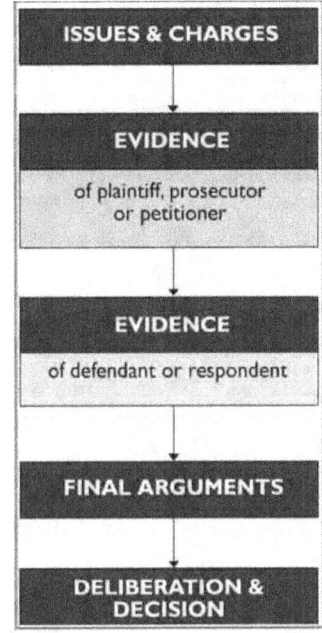

tions focus on improving the speed of oral proceedings, facilitating the effective presentation of evidence, and ensuring the quality of records made of those proceedings. Courts need adequate facilities and support services to conduct oral hearings. They need systems for (1) recording what is said; (2) recording hearing outcomes, such as court procedural orders, and providing documented proof of those orders; (3) formally presenting oral evidence to the judge; (4) electronic evidence presentation; and (5) storing and managing documents and other evidentiary material given to the court during a hearing.

Recording oral proceedings. Some courts still record proceedings by shorthand, typewriter/computer, or stenotype machine. Courts with more advanced management systems use electronic digital audio systems to record courtroom hearings. The resulting oral record is clear and in searchable format. This approach requires that courtrooms have microphones and amplification systems operated by a trained employee. In addition to ensuring the accuracy, completeness, and objectivity of the record, sound recording discourages misbehavior during hearings and reduces the prospect of official court records being altered or destroyed.

"NAG CLERKS." Since 2005, in South Africa, a support clerk for court administration in criminal matters, known as the "nag clerk," has assisted the magistrate and prosecutor's office to make sure that all related procedures and people are ready and that proper steps have been completed. This is a full-time paralegal-level position. The individual tracks all parties to confirm attendance on the scheduled dates and checks that all paperwork has been submitted as required, in addition to handling all auxiliary needs to guarantee that the docket schedule is met. This "nagging" reduces delays and adjournments resulting from parties not being prepared or not showing up, and it keeps the trials moving along in a timely manner.

Transcript. It usually costs much less to produce a sound recording of court proceedings than to produce a verbatim transcript manually. However, this cost advantage is often lost if a verbatim transcript must then be produced from the sound recording. Effectively managed courts maintain the economy of sound recording by avoiding the need to produce a verbatim transcript wherever possible.

Non-judicial court personnel in adjudication. Effective management of hearings and trials requires a range of skilled courtroom personnel. These include:

- **Sound recording operators** (or stenotype or keyboard stenographers) to record what is said

- **Transcription typists** to produce transcripts from sound recordings or a stenotype record, usually in a location away from the courtroom

- **Court clerks** to manage court records and process documentary evidence offered in court

- **Judicial attendants** to act as a

FACTORS TO CONSIDER IN PROJECT DESIGN

Does the court provide adequate courtroom facilities for recording hearings and producing transcripts?

Does the court sound-record its proceedings?

What features of courtrooms and personnel enhance and/or impede the effectiveness of oral hearings?

---

personal assistant to each judge during a hearing

- **Judicial secretaries** to manage a judge's office or chamber and to arrange the typing of written judgments

- **Evidence presentation operators** to operate audiovisual equipment used to present evidence

- **Database operators** in cases where evidence is presented electronically from an in-court computerized database

- **Courtroom orderlies** to maintain order, usher witnesses and litigants, and assist advocates who are addressing the court

- **Security officers**, sheriff officers, or court police to assure courtroom and judicial security

H. PUBLICATION, REVIEW, AND ENFORCEMENT OF COURT DECISIONS – PHASES 7-9

These phases occur after the trial is over. Effectively managed courts:

- Publish their decisions, complete with argument, ideally using the Internet

- Have clear processes for enforcing their decisions and minimizing the use of oral judicial hearings

- Use a variety of enforcement options

- Apply processes that minimize parties' opportunities to frustrate or delay the enforcement of court decisions by appeal or review

- Use specialized court personnel to administer enforcement processes

Varying levels of publication of judicial decisions. Courts that have not undergone modernization or reform tend not to publish their decisions except for the benefit of the parties and enforcement authorities. In recent years, many courts have adopted policies supporting the broad publication of court decisions. The purposes are to promote greater transparency and to foster the development of the law through improved consistency of decisions. This change is being driven by (1) increased public interest in gaining access to public information held by state agencies, such as under freedom of information laws, and (2) improved technology that enables courts to provide access to case information relatively inexpensively via the Internet. These developments have encouraged courts to acquire the capacity to produce decisions in searchable electronic format as a means of granting access. To facilitate electronic access, courts are increasingly relying on word-processing and associated electronic information management systems to administer their core processes. (These systems also support the compilation of statistical data on caseloads and judicial productivity to enhance court management overall.)

Non-judicial court personnel in publishing decisions. In courts that have automated the production, duplication, and distribution of court decisions, adoption of new systems requires new skills on the part of court staff and therefore greater investment in preparing existing staff to assume these new and more complex functions. It also requires adding new professional and quasi-professional positions to the staff required to operate the courts. In many courts without automation, when someone requests a

Figure 12. Levels of Publication of Court Decisions

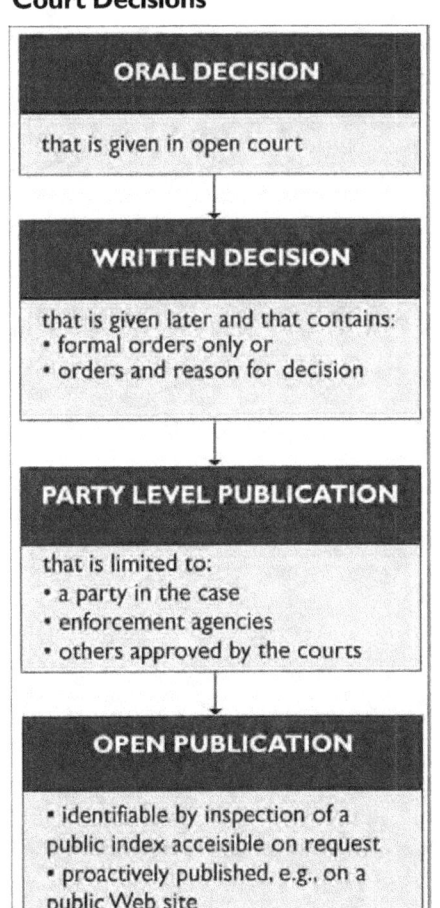

copy of a decision, clerical registry personnel provide it manually. Where the decision is published electronically, staff may respond using dedicated information and communications systems, such as by delivery to a Web site or by e-mail. Figure 12 illustrates the different levels of publication that a court may use.

Appeal, review, and re-litigation. Some court systems allow wide opportunities for those with judgments against them or those convicted of offenses to appeal the decision. Effective courts avoid excessive appeals and related bureaucratic paperwork by providing efficient systems for processing appeals and other applications aimed at avoiding or delaying court orders. Strategies include limiting the scope of appeals, limiting the time in which an appeal may be filed, and offering fast-track mechanisms for deciding appeals and reviewing applications.

Enforcement of court decisions. Effective courts need enforcement mechanisms that do not encourage defiance or avoidance of court orders. In many court systems throughout the world, particularly those in many former communist countries, processes for enforcing civil court orders to pay money or to forfeit assets are poorly developed. Courts in those systems commonly complain that enforcement of civil judgments against powerful institutions, such as government agencies, is voluntary because the formal coercive powers of the courts are inadequate or non-existent.

Non-judicial court personnel in enforcement. In many court systems, enforcement of a judgment is labor-intensive. The application for enforcement of a court order is scheduled for an oral hearing, and notice is served on the other party. Effectively managed courts, however, use systems that minimize the referral of enforce-

FACTORS TO CONSIDER IN PROJECT DESIGN

Does the court have efficient systems for producing its decisions?

Does the court have clearly defined policies and procedures governing access to, and publication of, its decisions?

Does the court minimize opportunities for frivolous appeals?

How effectively are the court's decisions enforced?

Chapter Summary

ment processes to judicial oral hearings or otherwise demand significant judicial effort. Instead, these courts delegate enforcement tasks to non-judicial court personnel. Although arrest and imprisonment require direct judicial involvement, other enforcement mechanisms require very little, if any, judicial effort. The types of court personnel that may conduct enforcement include:

- **Court bailiffs** to administer asset-seizure processes

- **Court administrators** to manage special court staff units that issue, service, and administer third-party enforcement orders

- **Registrars** to administer hearings in which judgment debtors may be examined and questioned about the nature and location of their assets

In addition, legislation may establish special agencies outside courts to enforce particular kinds of court orders, such as traffic fines.

Understanding the court functions required for case adjudication is essential to the design of effective rule of law programs that improve court operations. Non-judicial court personnel provide essential support to the nine phases of case adjudication, from case initiation through enforcement of judgments. As more courts adopt caseflow management principles, more staff with a wider range of skills are needed to assist judges in every phase. Rule of law programs that promote better use of these personnel and enhance their performance can:

- Increase court efficiency

- Advance transparency

- Capitalize on new technologies

- Improve the quality of justice

- Reduce opportunities for corruption

V. COURT PERSONNEL REFORM: PROJECT IMPLEMENTATION

This chapter identifies strategies and approaches that promote success in court personnel and management reform projects. It also highlights considerations in selecting from among reform options and presents good practices that can be replicated and/or refined in various settings.

A. GENERAL PRINCIPLES: SUCCESS FACTORS AND RISKS IN COURT PERSONNEL REFORM PROGRAMS

Court personnel and management reform programming requires consideration of a range of needs. These needs include:

- Executive branch buy-in
- Judicial branch buy-in
- Buy-in from all other stakeholders
- Multi-level legal and policy reform
- Planning and sequencing
- Adequate funding
- Realism and sustainability

Executive branch buy-in. Reforming judicial and court systems implies strengthening a branch of government whose goal in pursuing the rule of law may not always coincide with that of the executive branch. In fact, achieving an independent judiciary may not be an executive branch priority at all. Although a foreign donor cannot play a constructive role in disputes between a judiciary and its government, especially on issues of judicial independence, it can advance projects related to court administration systems and personnel reform. This is because court efficiency and effectiveness are non-political. However, even with these projects, consensus building is essential to prevent intra-governmental disputes or delays due to competing interests of government agencies. The Ministry of Justice and other relevant portions of the executive branch need to support the reform on all levels, given their role in coordinating court management and administration.

Judicial branch buy-in. Judicial and court reform programs are frequently sanctioned by the executive branch on behalf of the nation and the judiciary. This formality belies the importance of true consent and commitment from the judiciary itself. In environments where the judiciary and the executive branch are in conflict, the extent of judicial commitment to a reform program may be sharply at odds with that of the executive branch. The judiciary may oppose a proposed program or have differing expectations for it. Some judiciaries are subservient to the executive or have a hostile relationship with it. In these situations, the consent of a judiciary led by judges willing to follow executive direction may be of little value if there is no consent by the broader judiciary.

Another potential risk is the absence of judicial commitment to or understanding of the objectives of a court reform project. Successful projects address these barriers early, in the planning and development stages.

The highest court authority must take an active leadership role in implementing the project and must regularly communicate his/her support throughout the judicial system. This support needs to be echoed by the highest court authority in the region or regions of implementation. In the Philippines, the guidance and leadership of the Supreme Court Chief Justice facilitated widespread judicial support, even if the reform resulted in the relinquishing of certain judicial powers.

Buy-in from all other stakeholders. Court reform project designs need input and buy-in from all of the other relevant stakeholders, beyond the executive and judicial branches. This ensures that the design addresses a broad range of concerns and divergent perspectives. Broad stakeholder consensus averts later clashes over judicial powers and responsibilities. It also helps establish feasible timelines, create realistic expectations of all actors, and facilitate national ownership of the project.

Non-judicial leadership and support play an important role in driving and sustaining reform processes. Individuals in key positions in civil society, non-governmental organizations including the bar, and academia can provide essential support for the project. They can collaborate closely with each other and with the judicial leadership to facilitate public awareness and to mobilize outside resources to advance the project goals.

Donors are also stakeholders. In many countries, multiple donors work on court reform simultaneously. Lack of buy-in through donor coordination may result in redundancies and contradictions in the reform initiative, particularly when donors represent different legal traditions.

Multi-level legal and policy reform. Court personnel and management reform may require legislative change, the creation of new government offices, and the realignment of powers within the Ministry of Justice and judicial branch. These changes may in turn require legislative reform and constitutional amendments. Court reform project designs should account for these types of legal and political changes.

Planning and sequencing. Planning and contracting for project implementation can take years. During the lead time, factors affecting implementation can change. For example, a change in the executive branch or in the judicial leadership can increase or decrease commitment before the project has even begun. Nevertheless, it is risky to launch and design a project too quickly. Moreover, the project time frame must be adequate to implement reform, while also allowing for generating stakeholder buy-in.

Sequencing of project components is equally important. Activities in supporting legislative reform, legal training, and new court administration systems must be phased, synchronized, and meshed with each other in an overall strategy because they are inter-related.

Adequate funding. A key factor for project success is securing adequate

funding, in advance, for completion of the entire project. Court reform projects are multi-year initiatives. Many involve both capital and human resource improvements and may require large initial investments in legislative reform and training of judicial system personnel. Funding for infrastructure is a key consideration since inadequate infrastructure can inhibit court capacity to provide the necessary services and thus limit the impact of reform. Funding for a pilot component only, without guaranteed support for a national rollout, will also limit project impact. Some pilot court projects may be doomed from the beginning because of gaps in available resources, systems, and personnel that the projects are not equipped to close.

Realism and sustainability. Successful projects generally target modest gains and use proven methods. Unrealistic court reform activities that are likely to fail jeopardize the achievement of reform goals. To increase the chances that the project will achieve its target results, the design must reflect a careful evaluation of the potential risks. Conducting an assessment helps determine whether the target reform is too widespread or extensive, and whether the results can be achieved within the desired timeline or budgetary allocation. Funding should be limited to those projects that can be sustained by local resources beyond the donor assistance phase.

FACTORS TO CONSIDER IN PROJECT DESIGN

Does your project have a strategy for assuring and preserving stakeholder buy-in?

Does your project have sufficient time, resources, and other critical elements to achieve target results? If not, what can project managers do to adjust the objectives or to strengthen the commitment to achieving them?

B. COMPONENTS OF COURT REFORM PROGRAMS

The components of court reform programs fall into three programmatic areas (Figure 13):

- Strategic policy reform
- Skills and knowledge development
- Court business, court systems, and infrastructure reform

Figure 13. Components of Court

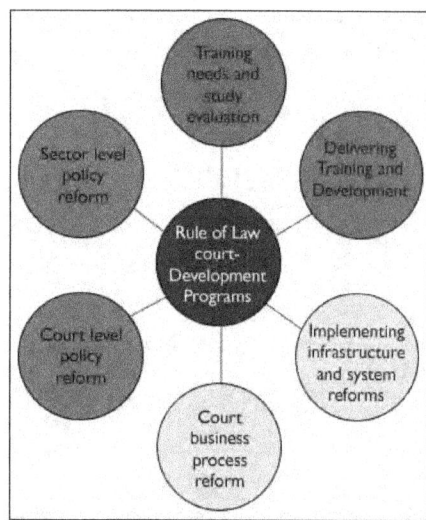

Most court personnel and management reform projects contain all three components in varying degrees. The rest of this chapter is organized by component to illustrate what these projects do and how they do it most successfully.

Court personnel and management reform projects seek to achieve change (for example, in how responsibilities are aligned, how elements of the justice system are organized, and how work is done.) Projects must clearly articulate the desired reform, select feasible strategies to achieve it, and incorporate an iterative process for on-going review, adjustment, and correction. This process includes (1) developing (or reviewing) the reform strategy, (2) selecting specific reform options, (3) testing the options, (4) evaluating the results, and (5) assessing the impact of implementation on the overall reform strategy.

C. STRATEGIC POLICY REFORM

Court reform programming needs to take into account, and ideally influence, the development of high-level policy because policy affects how courts are managed. Strategic policy reform activities can:

- Develop national-level strategies for court system managerial reform

- Support legislative reform programs that affect court processes

- Address system-wide managerial challenges by (1) increasing court budgets, (2) providing for central offices of court administration, and (3) resolving structural features that impair court effectiveness

Assessing needs for strategic policy reform. Most court reform projects require major policy and structural changes. Because all judicial systems have unique features, a needs assessment can help define these requirements and determine the project's possible role in meeting them.

Developing national judicial reform plans. A common goal in judicial reform programming is the development and adoption of system-wide reform action plans or strategies that specifically address the need for national-level reform. Donors often support the development of these plans. Once adopted by the judiciary with the support of the executive branch or legislature, they provide a solid authority for advancing the agendas of rule of law programs. Macedonia's National Justice Strategy reform program addressed both legislative and administrative reform of the court system. The

Supreme Court of the Philippines adopted a six-year plan known as the *Action Program for Judicial Reform,* which has been the vehicle for a range of donor-funded court improvement programs. The Supreme Court of Indonesia adopted a range of blueprints for judicial reform. These are comparable to the Philippines action plan in terms of scope, duration, and value in facilitating donor programs. Similar plans have been adopted in Mongolia and some Latin American countries.

Supporting legislative drafting and reform. Because strategic policy reform occurs at the highest level, effective programming often requires first meeting with legislative leaders and then ensuring that they are included in all major deliberations. This approach is essential in former communist countries that are committed to developing modern market economies. The reason is that legislators in these countries generally have a keen interest in reforms that help to boost the confidence of the international investment community. Such reforms may require fundamental adjustments to essential laws and state institutions as a prerequisite to effective court system development. Frequently, a necessary first step in reform is supporting the legislative change process. This process can produce near complete statutory reforms affecting courts and their administration. To support statutory reform, project activities include the following:

- **Outreach.** Given buy-in requirements, it is critical for USAID officials and contractors to meet and work with legislative leaders who oversee the judicial system.

- **Facilitating drafting meetings.** Projects can benefit from coordinating regular meetings or consultations of legislators, judicial system officials, local legal experts, bar representatives, Ministry of Finance

staff, and even members of civil society. The objective is to involve judicial system leaders and a broad range of stakeholders in drafting laws that will impact the finances, staffing, training, and functions of the courts.

- **Using local legal experts.** Local constitutional and legislative experts can be invaluable in identifying which laws and statutes need to be amended and in navigating the amendment process.

> **LEGISLATIVE REFORM IN MACEDONIA**
>
> The judiciary and the government of the Republic of Macedonia received technical assistance in legal policy reform research, reform advocacy, and legal drafting. This assistance resulted in government and judicial consensus in developing a national justice strategy that produced new statutes. These statutes impacted the structure of the judiciary, provided reforms to criminal and civil procedure, and brought about improvements in law enforcement systems. The results were achieved by (1) providing skilled Macedonian lawyers to assist directly with research, consultations, and the drafting of proposed laws, and (2) fostering public consultation that assured the participation of the judiciary, the legislature, the executive, and the general public in negotiating a statutory reform program. A key success factor was the transparency of the process, which encouraged the executive and the judiciary to consult – with each other and all stakeholders – before committing to reforms that could be resisted by those who might otherwise have been excluded from the process.

Deficiencies in court budgets and their management. In most developing countries, court improvement requires increasing the courts' operating budget and improving budget management. Often, court budget deficiencies are dramatic, making advocacy for more funding a high-level operational priority for the court system. In the strategic policy reform area, donor projects empower court systems to meet this challenge by helping counterparts to demonstrate the extent of budget deficiencies and to frame effective budget proposals. To persuade the executive and legislative leadership that courts need more money, these proposals must document the need. They must also show that the money invested is worthwhile by demonstrating impact and measurable results. Strategic policy reform activities can address the following budget-related issues:

- **Financial control.** Assisting court personnel to manage resources allocated to them more rigorously, including improved systems of accounting, controlling expenditure, and preventing the loss of funds through embezzlement or mismanagement

- **Asset management.** Assisting in evaluating court assets and the adequacy of asset management systems, such as courthouse maintenance and management

- **Efficiency.** Supporting the quantification of court financial needs and the effects of budget shortages on the capacity of courts to dispose of their caseloads. In developing countries, allocating additional funding to the judiciary may not be possible because the government's resources are limited. An alternative is to examine opportunities to cut costs and reduce waste.

- **Ensuring equitable salaries.** The largest cost item in a court budget is usually salaries. To establish the judiciary as a priority, the legislature

must guarantee salaries, and judicial salaries must be comparable to those of other public office holders. Installing civil service status and professional salaries for the non-judicial court personnel attracts more competent staff. However, adequate salaries must be complemented with evidence that judges are at work and working hard. Legislators sometimes express reservations about judicial productivity and receive complaints from their constituents that judges are not always on the job during normal working hours.

- **Budget advocacy.** Assisting in preparing and justifying budget proposals

- **Coordination.** Advocates for budget increases for the courts need positive and ongoing relationships with legislative representatives who oversee the justice system. There is often little or no interaction between legislative and judicial officials. The result is that no one in the legislature is in a position to argue for the judicial system's resource re-

COURT BUDGETS IN THE PHILIPPINES

The Supreme Court of the Philippines has devoted considerable lobbying and advocacy effort to convince the government and the public that the courts need substantially more funding. For example, drawing on detailed research, the court has forcefully argued in a variety of publications that there are too few judges for the population, and that the courts' share of funding is not only inadequate, but is also diminishing as a proportion of overall government expenditures. This vigorous effort has so far been largely fruitless, but it has succeeded in keeping the budget issue as a core concern of the judiciary and a recurring theme of public debate about the efficiency of the court system.

quirements. Projects can facilitate interaction by, for example, urging chief judges to invite local legislators to visit their courts and discuss their needs and seeing that legislators are invited to participate in special court functions at which they receive recognition. Far too often, court personnel neglect these important relationships, and court budgets suffer the consequences.

Court management offices and administrators. Many court systems cannot develop policy on behalf of the whole system because there is no adequately empowered judicial system policy-making function in a senior judicial council and because there are no senior court administrator cadres. Establishing an administrative office for court management is a mainstay of many projects with strategic policy reform components, especially those sponsored by USAID. Success requires first carefully defining what mechanisms already are in effect, the extent of their control, and who operates and maintains them.

Offices of court administration, headed by executives who are primarily accountable to the judiciary, are an important feature of U.S. state and federal court structures. These offices are credited with driving system-wide U.S. reform for court budget management, personnel administration, and asset management. Western European systems have developed similar capacities via state ministries of justice, which are often staffed by seconded career judges, prosecutors, and other personnel who serve judicial needs. In contrast, in many developing countries, executive branch officials have policy and administrative authority over the judicial system. However, donor-assisted programs have recently successfully established this capacity in several countries. Examples include: (1) the pioneering efforts of the Hungarian government in the late 1990s in establishing the Administrative Bureau under the direction of the Judicial Council; (2) the Macedonia National Justice Strategy reform program that entailed establishing by statute an Administrative Office of the Court Budget Council with features closely resembling U.S. court administration offices; and (3) establishment in the Philippines of a Program Management Office to drive a specific reform program and avoid the inefficiencies and resistance of a very hierarchical, rigid court administration structure.

COMBATING WASTE OF POSTAGE IN SERBIA

The courts in Serbia were spending large portions of their budgets on postage costs associated with delivering notices of service and process. All notices went out by registered mail with return receipt, which is very costly. Through negotiation with the postal service under threat of outsourcing the substantial business of the delivery service, postal officials agreed to reduce costs significantly. The savings were diverted to other critical court system functions.

Developing these kinds of offices has high value because it establishes formal and sustainable organizations that can act as drivers of reform beyond the life of the assistance program. Projects can support the introduction of a judicial council, administrative office of the courts, program management office, and/or chief court administrator.

Systemic structural reform. Taking a broad strategic view can result in significant structural changes that affect the scale and diversity of a court system and its resulting administrative needs. Legislative changes that alter the structure of the court system, the work of courts, or the relationship of general courts to other tribunals can significantly impact the courts' adminis-

trative and operational priorities as well as their capacities. Projects supporting strategic policy reform can resolve numerous systemic inefficiencies, including the following:

- **Structural imbalances.** Imbalances or mismatches in the number, type, or geographic accessibility of appellate and trial courts

- **Courts within courts.** Special courts or tribunals within the administration of general courts that entail separate judicial appointments and separate processes of adjudication and registry services

- **Antiquated enforcement processes.** Lack of systems for enforcing civil court judgments or enforcement systems that require judges to perform sometimes onerous and inefficient non-adjudicative functions

- **Ineffective legislative reforms.** Legislation that is aimed at remedy-

---

FACTORS TO CONSIDER IN PROJECT DESIGN

Does your project consider high-level strategic reform options affecting the court system?

Are there structural or legislative factors that pose significant risks to achieving target results? If so, what measures can your project take to address those risks?

Does the court system have a strategy for improving its budgetary position? What impact does that strategy, or the lack thereof, have on the potential sustainability of project activities?

Does the court system have a central office of court management or equivalent? If not, are its leaders supportive of an effort to establish such a centralized administrative authority under the supervision of a judicial council?

---

ing specific social problems, but may effectively increase, rather than reduce, the number of prosecutions or civil disputes in courts

D. SKILLS AND KNOWLEDGE DEVELOPMENT

To develop court personnel, projects support the following:

- Assessing training needs (who needs to be trained and in what)

- Delivering training

- Developing information materials and tools that develop and sustain skills, knowledge, and other capacities

The prevalence of training objectives. Most court reform programs have at least one component -- often a major one -- dedicated to training and development of court personnel. The following text box illustrates how three court reform projects incorporated training into their objectives.

Potential pitfalls in training programming. Training of court personnel can be appealing because it is in many ways easier to implement than other activities, such as strategic reform, introducing operational changes, or technology procurement. On this basis, implementing organizations frequently substitute training programs for other, more difficult project work. It is critical first to understand the functional infrastructure of courts and their operating practices to identify what improvements and changes are needed. What may appear at first to be a training problem often is not, and the most sophisticated and costly training effort will fail to address it. Training can address a limited range of institutional reform challenges. Defining the problem is essential before determining that training is the appropriate response.

For all kinds of reasons, training sometimes results in failure to improve the court system. In many countries, court personnel are not well educated and have few resources, thus making it difficult to absorb and use training. Even where personnel are ready for training, it can be difficult to demonstrate that improvements result from the training. Numerous other factors, associated with training design and methodology, trainee selection, and conditions within the system to which trainees return, can affect training impact. All these issues need attention in deciding if, when, and how to use training in court personnel and management reform projects.

I. ASSESSING NEEDS

Is an assessment needed? Failure to assess training needs adequately before offering training can result in targeting the wrong recipients for training or designing training that is too simple or too complicated for the target trainees. It also makes it difficult to establish and justify clear training goals, and to evaluate the success of training programs. Therefore, undertaking a formal and carefully designed training needs assessment (TNA) should be a high priority for any court personnel and management reform project concerned with training.

Data sources and collection methods. A TNA gathers data to define gaps between existing and desired competencies. Data sources include (1) court staff surveys; (2) surveys of or consultations with court users (parties, witnesses, lawyers, other advocates, and the general public); (3) training committees, if any, comprised of court personnel; (4) observations of court operations; (5) review of training requests by court personnel; and (6) secondary sources, such as existing records of complaints by court users and of cases overturned, sent back, or otherwise mishandled.

Survey instruments should be carefully designed and tested. For example, for court staff, the survey should develop information on existing skills and knowledge related to the court's functions rather than the staff's perception of training needs or the topics on which they would like to receive training.

PROGRAM OBJECTIVES
Russian-American Judicial Partnership, 2001 onwards (USAID)

1. Expand and improve judicial training capabilities.

2. Improve judicial administration capabilities.

3. Heighten judges' awareness of ethics.

Macedonia Court Modernization Project, 2002–2007 (USAID)

1. Improve legal structures and practices.

2. Improve court administration and management.

3. Improve legal training.

Mongolia Judicial Reform Program, 2001–2005 (World Bank)

1. Strengthen court administration and case management.

2. Establish a unified information system.

3. Improve standards at the Mongolian law schools and faculties.

4. Establish a standardized and continuing legal education system.

5. Design and implement legal qualifying standards.

6. Improve the coordination and clarify lines of duties of justice system agencies.

TRAINING NEEDS ASSESSMENT (TNA)

- TNA helps court reform projects:

- Match training content with the business priorities of the court, filling the gaps that prevent the court from achieving its goals

- Identify the current skills, knowledge, and abilities of existing personnel

- Assess and rank how various training options will likely improve performance

- Verify that training, rather than other interventions, will contribute significantly to closing performance gaps

- Test training content to evaluate the potential return and ascertain the risks involved

---

SURVEYING USER OPINION IN COLOMBIA

The municipal Itagui courts in the city of Medellin, Colombia, survey the opinions of court users every six months. The surveys cover lawyers' opinions on information services, document processing, the times spent in providing services, user needs, numbers of people served, peak service periods, and principal user profiles. A judicial committee routinely reviews the results of each survey and uses them to justify and defend procedural improvement proposals. Surveys have also driven the development and provision of staff training and community education programs in which Itagui judges have directly addressed local community groups on legal and procedural issues. Not only have public surveys assisted in capturing information for self-evaluation purposes, they have also become a principal engine for generating new ideas for improving court services at Itagui.

As training progresses, additional sources of data for an iterative TNA include evaluations conducted after each training session, pre- and post-training tests, and formal or informal consultations with judges, other court staff, and/or users regarding the performance of those who have been trained.

2. DELIVERING TRAINING

Developing judicial and non-judicial personnel. Project training budgets have disproportionately targeted training for judges. Because non-judicial personnel are so essential to court operations, effective court reform projects must provide for training them as well. All programs need to use adult learning methodologies.

Training institution development. Court reform projects often develop or support the local institutions that are responsible either for judicial and court administration training or for general legal training. Many USAID programs operate in countries with institutional mechanisms for judicial training, such as judicial councils or academies established by statute or within ministries of justice. In Macedonia, for example, a special Academy for Judges and Prosecutors was established in 2006 with the encouragement and active support of a USAID-sponsored rule of law program. Project assistance to such institutions can include:

- Improving institutional governance by mentoring directors and other senior personnel

- Supporting the development of processes for TNAs, curriculum design, and promotion of training programs

- Developing full-time and part-time faculty by offering training-of-trainer courses and curriculum documentation

- Funding courses provided by faculty

- Developing computerized databases for managing trainee records and course programming

Training judges. In addition to curricula offered by in-country training institutions, topical seminars, periodic seminars, and annual judicial conferences are venues for training judges in new procedures and other changes and innovations associated with court personnel and management reform. Study tours to courts in other countries, attendance at international conferences, and intensive special training courses on topics of particular interest to donors, such as human rights law, environmental law, and criminal prosecution procedural reform are also beneficial but serve small numbers of participants. Also, they often require special donor funding.

Special joint training for judges and other court personnel. These kinds of programs can reach large numbers of court system personnel. In the Philippines, for example, a drive to reduce corruption was facilitated by a major nationwide training program in 2005 for judges and other court personnel. The objective was to promote newly developed judicial codes of conduct. Programs of this kind can be very effective in facilitating behavioral change when used in conjunction with other reform activities. The Philippines program was complemented by an upgraded judicial complaints system that permitted more effective monitoring and detection of judicial corruption, a feature that made the training program more relevant to participants. The Philippines approach is less likely to be successful when training about ethical conduct is offered without any complementary initiatives.

Training non-judicial court personnel. Court reform projects often focus on developing capacity within a court to offer non-judicial staff training routinely. Because of the diversity of

responsibilities among these staff, the range of training topics is broad. Also, in contrast to registrars and other senior staff, clerical officers, bailiffs, and others may have limited education and be less accustomed to organized instruction or study. TNAs for particular classes of court personnel will define these differences and direct the use of more appropriate training techniques. Techniques can include:

- On-the-job mentoring programs by which staff learn under the formalized guidance of a supervisor

- Classroom or seminar training sessions on specific tasks required to conduct the court's business

- Computer skills and applications training, using classroom methods or computer-aided training software

The last two techniques are commonly used in conjunction with the reform of court business processes. In addition, developing procedure manuals for specific tasks (for example, for process serving) can support formal training and also serve as a continuing resource on the job.

It is also important to raise competencies among non-judicial court personnel in areas other than their core tasks. These personnel can play important roles in assisting judges in managing cases and in relieving them of other tasks that limit judicial productivity, such as court management. The more professional they are, the more they can strengthen the court's capacity. Projects can support skills training in team building, supervision and management, change management, and court planning.

3. DEVELOPING INFORMATION MATERIALS AND TOOLS

Information as a training and business tool. More and better structured information about the law and the work of the courts increases the competencies of judges and other court personnel. It also facilitates court administration. Structured information can support training as well as the conduct of court functions. Best practice activities include:

- Modernizing procedures guides

- Replenishing law libraries

- Improving access to legal information through technology

- Improving court business information tools and their use

- Promoting regional information sharing and cooperation

Modernizing procedures guides.
The traditional training tool of courts is a book commonly called the rules of court. These can be quite extensive, amounting in complex systems to thousands of pages. Lengthy and out-of-date court rules can impede the development of skills and court reform activities generally. The reason is that court rules may govern court activities so completely that they either prevent specific procedural changes or prohibit any changes that are not expressly authorized in the rules. Court reform projects must often support modernizing court rules as a prerequisite to implementing specific procedural reforms. Court rules are often the only procedures manual available to court person-

nel. Therefore, they are the starting point in developing new procedures manuals. Many court reform projects engage court personnel in revising procedures and developing new manuals.

Replenishing law libraries. Developing judicial competencies requires building up law libraries that are accessible to judges. Essential texts, such as statutes and regulations, are unavailable to judges in many systems, forcing judges to use their own resources to inform themselves about the law. This can degrade the skill of judges over time, impede the efficiency of adjudication, have a detrimental effect on the quality of decisions and thus the quality of justice, and increase judicial dependency on regular training. Court reform projects can address this problem by procuring statutes, law reports, and legal periodicals that judges can use. This approach is often more efficient and sustainable than continuous and relatively expensive judicial training programs.

Improving access to legal information through technology.

REINSTATING THE RULE OF LAW IN AFGHANISTAN
The USAID rule of law project in Afghanistan has devoted substantial resources to compiling the laws, regulations, and official government gazettes of Afghanistan and translating them into English and Afghan languages.

Although this work included using computers to make this information more accessible, the act of compiling and printing indices of the laws alone was sufficient to justify the effort. The primary benefit was substantially to reinstate the transparency of laws, an essential first step in reacquainting a post-war community, including its own judiciary and legal profession, with the rule of law.

The cost of supplying and maintaining statutes, law books, and other paper materials to keep judges informed is high. Therefore, some court reform projects assist courts in transitioning to electronic systems. This reduces compilation and distribution costs, but it also assumes that court users have access to affordable information technology. In many court systems, access is increasing as they acquire information technology infrastructure for other purposes, such as managing and using information about the court's business.

Options for electronic access include supplying information through CD-ROM and DVD disks or via web-accessible databases. The first option is more expensive than on-line access, but still costs less than producing than paper materials. However, web-accessible databases also present challenges. Few succeed completely because of logistical and sustainability problems. Although the concept of these databases and the planned methods for maintaining them may be sound, initiatives can falter because of deficiencies in technical infrastructure, shortages of technically competent personnel, and failure to plan for sustaining the costs. Nonetheless, where they do succeed the benefits can be substantial, not only for the judiciary, but also for the public. Activities with low investment and high potential impact include facilitating online or database access to:

- Court decisions

- Legal research materials

- Legal commentaries

- Procedural and substantive codes and laws

Improving court business information tools and their use. Court personnel need access to relevant information on the business of courts, such as case management and admini-

BUSINESS TRAINING
In South Africa, the training for court managers has a substantial focus on practical business and executive skills, and it employs leadership building activities. This training enables the managers to administer the courts more effectively and to be leaders in developing reform.

stration, file management, process serving, or court revenue management. They also need the capacity to interpret statistics and use them. Courts generally collect statistics of various kinds and compile them into reports that support decisions about case management and administration. A sudden spike in case filings in a given month, for example, can indicate an imminent increase in hearings.

Improving court business information tools and their use.

U.S. TRIAL COURT PERFORMANCE STANDARDS

In 1990, the U.S. National Center for State Courts helped develop a *Trial Courts Performance Standards and Measurement System*, which is comprehensive and is kept up to date. These very detailed standards, however, do not translate readily to developing court systems because they were intended specifically for U.S. courts and assume U.S. standards of court personnel competencies and resources. Nonetheless, they offer an excellent reference for court reform programs. The standards can be viewed online at http://www.ncsconline.org/ D_Research/tcps/index.html.

Court personnel need access to relevant information on the business of courts, such as case management and administration, file management, process serving, or court revenue manage-

ONLINE LEGAL INFORMATION IN ALBANIA

The World Bank's Legal and Judicial Reform Project in Albania faced many difficulties in implementation, but the dissemination of legal information component was successful. The project developed a computerized, Internet-accessible database for supreme court decisions and a similar database for Albanian legislation.

ment. They also need the capacity to interpret statistics and use them. Courts generally collect statistics of various kinds and compile them into reports that support decisions about case management and administration. A sudden spike in case filings in a given month, for example, can indicate an imminent increase in hearings.

More and more courts are acquiring

SUPPORT FROM AREA COURT MANAGERS

In South Africa, court managers are grouped in clusters, typically comprising six to eight managers. These court managers serve under a full-time area court manager, who is responsible for their coordination, communication, and oversight. The area court managers set goals and measure achievements of each court to ensure accountability and the highest level of performance. The area court managers are successful in applying pressure on court managers to meet their court performance goals and in evaluating whether goals have been met.

computers to store and manage information. Court personnel need skills not only in basic computer operations, but also in interpreting information and using it to make decisions. Many court reform projects provide this training. They also provide assistance in structuring information so that courts can accurately define and measure their functions and processes. Some projects focus on establishing case management statistical and performance indicator analysis as a technique for reducing delays and backlog and on training court staff in that technique. There are general benchmarks that effective courts use to measure their key business processes. Examples include (1) court workloads, (2) the causes of case backlog, (3) the nature and extent of court delays, and (4) the effects and

effectiveness of court adjudication processes.

Promoting regional information sharing and cooperation. Courts within a designated region (or appellate circuit) can benefit from sharing information and best practices. These consultations may involve judges, court managers, or chief judge-administrators meeting regularly to discuss court administration and management issues. They can foster innovation and a willingness to experiment with new practices. They also facilitate opportunities to visit other courts and to see how those courts handle their functions. Further, regional consultations promote more consistent practices among area courts.

FACTORS TO CONSIDER IN PROJECT DESIGN

Does your project include a training component? If so, has a formal TNA been conducted?

Does the training component include both judicial and non-judicial personnel?

What training methods are used? How were they selected and justified in relation to the project's training goals?

Does your project supplement training with activities that develop information materials and tools?

E. BUSINESS PROCESSES AND SYSTEMS REFORM

In addressing business processes and systems reform, court reform projects support (1) pilot courts that test innovations and (2) personnel administration reform initiatives.

1. PILOT COURTS

Controlled testing through piloting. Many projects use a pilot court approach to develop and test reforms and new practices, such as improvements in court management, prior to replication and national roll-out. The size of the pilot can vary, from one court to multiple courts. To improve court performance, most pilots focus on court processes and services and on the tools, procedures, and facilities court personnel use. Target results typically include:

- Increasing the transparency and efficiency of court services

- Better meeting the needs of litigants and the general public

- Reducing backlogs of cases awaiting disposal

- Reducing delays that cases suffer up to disposal

- Reducing corruption and inefficiencies that facilitate corruption by improving transparency

---

WHERE TO FOCUS PILOT COURT PROGRAMS

A pilot program in South Africa was focused in one region and proved to be very successful, providing a model for the rest of the country. However, one complaint was that much of the rest of the country's courts did not benefit from the pilot. Although pilot programs in one region can provide an incubator for a successful project, spreading the project among multiple regions at the same time facilitates widespread impact.

A successful pilot lays the foundation for and justifies investments in expansion. Examples of pilot court activities include:

- Backlog reduction processing

- Case tracking computerization programs

- Other new technology

- Facilities improvement

- Establishing alternative dispute resolution

Backlog reduction processing. Many USAID rule of law programs encourage the adoption of caseflow management principles to reduce backlog. Applying caseflow management techniques requires courts to (1) identify and track cases that are outside acceptable standards of case delay, and (2) give priority attention to those cases so that they can be more quickly disposed. Project implementers typically facilitate the agreement by pilot court judges to adopt and test changes in trial and pre-trial procedures. Changes can relate to case preparation, settlement processes, and adjudicative hearings. One approach is to establish a backlog reduction committee, comprised of the pilot court judicial leadership. The committee regularly reviews each case awaiting disposal and examines options to expedite its disposal, such as by additional court sittings or by diversion processes like settlement or mediation. Backlog reduction committees established in several pilot courts under the USAID Macedonian Court Modernization Project had a significant impact on reducing backlog, largely by providing more judicial attention to backlog cases that might otherwise have languished.

Many projects pilot test improved records processing to reduce backlog. They strengthen records management by redesigning the records themselves to facilitate better management. Activities can involve introducing or upgrading case record file covers, the official court registers, index books, and systems for physical storage. These simple improvements enable pilot courts to assert more control over the speed of record processing, record accuracy, and the range of accessible information about cases. USAID projects in Russia and Macedonia have demonstrated that modest records system improvements, even without the use of computerized technology, can contribute significantly to case management efficiency.

Case tracking computerization programs. Many projects use pilot courts to develop and test computerized case tracking and workflow management systems. These projects generally require significant hardware and software procurement as well as staff training in systems operation. However, hardware and software will not solve fundamental processing problems. Therefore, pilot projects must focus first on re-engineering court processes so that the computerized system, when introduced, truly increases efficiency.

Despite donor enthusiasm for funding the development of computer-assisted processes in courts, there are considerable challenges to implementation. USAID's rule of law program in Egypt introduced case tracking systems in two pilot courts in Cairo. The first phase of the pilot generated a number of important lessons:

- From the very start, host countries need to understand the costs of maintaining computer systems. Early on, they need to approve procedural changes required for automated case management.

- Court process re-engineering should occur prior to automation, be piloted first in small courts, and engage implementation committees in pilot courts.

- Court personnel involved in court process re-engineering should be selected on merit and trained in new systems as early as possible. Courts also need additional specialists to implement automated systems.

- Pilot projects should publicize the impact of new computerized systems among court users as changes occur.

Other new technology. Since 2001, the development of computerized systems for courts has progressed dramatically in terms of the range of things software can do and the impact that these capabilities can have on court services and practices. Not all case management systems are the same, and not all may be suitable for use in a pilot court. Figure 14 illustrates the expanding nature of technology use in courts and likely future directions, especially for highly developed court systems. Few courts in developing countries

court operations. Pilot court projects often commit substantial funds to improving facilities, such as judges' chambers, public reception areas, custodial facilities, document filing offices, and back-office areas for staff. USAID's Macedonia Court Modernization Project comprehensively refurbished several courthouses, aligning physical changes to complement changes in court procedure. For example, a single document filing area, called an intake center, was fitted out to render speedier public information and document filing services. This innovation helped both court personnel and the general public to recognize the value of reforming document filing procedures in those courthouses. The impact of courthouse layout changes can go beyond efficiency and access. As illustrated in Chapter 3, adding windows to the filing area can

Modifying case management processes to facilitate referral to mediation or other diversion processes

Measuring and evaluating the impact of mediation or similar processes on overall levels of litigation and case settlement

2. COURT PERSONNEL ADMINISTRATION SYSTEM REFORM

Initiatives in training, new information technology, case management process improvement, and judicial competencies development require ensuring and sustaining the caliber, motivation, and continuity of skilled non-judicial court personnel. To support these initiatives, court reform projects need to stimulate improvements in the overall management of personnel. Personnel management covers (1) selection and appointment, (2) remuneration, (3) promotion, (4) career development, (5) discipline and termination, (6) tenure, and (7) accountability and performance management. Many court reform projects have addressed personnel management for judges, but non-judicial personnel need similar attention. The reason is that better managed court staff can reinforce judicial independence and the judiciary's overall managerial effectiveness.

Figure 14. Stages of Information Technology Use in Courts

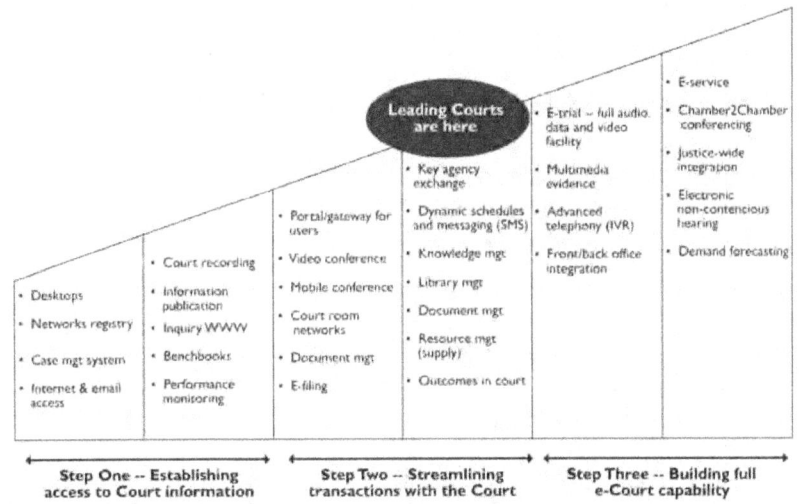

have reached even the first stage of this process. Thus, pilot court projects need to carefully define the intended goals in testing new technology and the likely implications for court personnel within that system.

Facilities improvement. The physical infrastructure of courts is often woefully inadequate in developing court systems. This has a negative impact on

markedly reduce corruption.

Establishing alternative dispute resolution. Pilot courts can test the implementation of new systems for alternative dispute resolution (ADR), such as court-annexed mediation schemes. These kinds of projects involve the following:

Training mediators and administrators

Improving non-judicial personnel administration. In most settings where USAID works, many factors challenge court personnel reform. These include nepotism, low-level corruption, poor standards of supervision, and a focus on employee entitlements rather than on obligations. Court management and personnel reform projects can address these factors and promote sustainable change by focusing on the following:

- **The merit principle.** Many USAID court reform projects establish chief executive and senior court administration positions. The reform process needs to include methods for filling these positions on the basis of merit, not nepotism. Selection must be competitive and fair.

- **Mobility.** Personnel systems need sufficient flexibility to permit rational, equitable movement of personnel from one position to another or from one location to another. Limitations on staff mobility or the use of transfer as an instrument to intimidate or enrich individuals have a negative effect on court personnel. Reforms in court personnel administration need to ensure that mobility is governed by the merit principle.

- **Adequate compensation.** The salaries of non-judicial personnel need to be commensurate with their responsibilities. When court reforms result in new personnel structures (for example, introducing court administrators), the budget needs to provide for adequate salaries that will attract qualified candidates and offer them an incentive to perform their duties. Low wages at the senior level relative to the judiciary or the broader public sector can jeopardize the discipline and integrity of court administrative staff.

- **Transparency of processes.** The culture of administrative personnel in courts can be secretive and defensive, serving the interests of the corrupt and inefficient. Courts need to emphasize transparency not only in court services, but also in the management of personnel. Projects can support the development of transparent processes for recruiting, hiring, evaluating, disciplining, and terminating staff. They can also support post-

ings in the media of standards, policies, and opportunities within the court to increase transparency.

- **Commitment to developing career personnel.** Some court systems give little recognition to the contribution that non-judicial personnel make. A sub-standard promotional and staff development system can produce workforces that are under-skilled, poorly paid, and seldom promoted. The development of professional positions, civil service status, professional organizations such as an association of court clerks, opportunities for promotion, and increased status help promote court personnel positions as career objectives. Court reform projects can support these initiatives.

- **Standards of conduct.** Many rule of law projects promote ethics among judges to reduce corruption in the judiciary. Non-judicial personnel need equal attention. Project approaches include developing codes of conduct, organizational planning programs, training programs, and inspection processes that define and enforce an ethical culture for court administrators.

FACTORS TO CONSIDER IN PROJECT DESIGN

Is your project developing pilot courts? If so, how much emphasis does it place on building the capacity of court personnel?

How is your project complementing capacity building activities with personnel administration reforms?

CHAPTER SUMMARY

Successful court personnel and management reform projects require a multi-tiered approach that impacts all aspects of the court system and its ad-

ministration, from the institutions that govern the judicial system to the skills and infrastructure within individual courts. Project designs must reflect a careful analysis of the deficiencies within the court system so that project interventions are appropriate and effective. Projects often include one or more of the following elements:

- Strategy and policy initiatives at the sector level and within courts (legislative changes, budgetary increases and improvements in financial management, and realignment of the court management structures)

- Skills and knowledge development (needs assessment, training, and improving access to legal and business information tools)

- Court business, infrastructure, and systems programming (through pilot court initiatives, improving human resource management policies, and introducing standards of conduct and transparency)

APPENDIX A

adversarial procedure	A procedure, developed chiefly within common law systems, under which courts allow advocates for the parties in a civil dispute or prosecution to define the questions in dispute and to select evidence for the court to consider. The role of judges is mainly to chair the proceedings, to listen to and read the evidence, and then to adjudicate.
alternative dispute resolution (ADR)	In relation to courts, ADR describes (1) any process that may be used as an alternative to traditional court case adjudication processes, and (2) dispute resolution processes that are concerned with negotiated settlement of cases of various types, including traditional elements of court processes, such as judicial conciliation
backlog	The accumulation of cases when case filings exceed case dispositions over a sustained period
calendar	A schedule of court hearings that indicates the assigned judge and court room
case delay	The failure of a case to be disposed or to reach some significant intermediate point within an acceptable time or a formal time standard
case adjudication	A process by which a court considers a case under a formal oral or documentary hearing procedure, normally resulting in a verdict and judgment of the court, finally determining the charges, dispute, or claim
case tracking	The process of monitoring the descriptive particulars of a case and the progression of formal events that apply to the case from filing to disposition
caseflow management	The proactive court monitoring and scheduling of cases to expedite case disposition within specified time periods. Caseflow management is concerned with coordinating court processes and resources so that groups of cases progress promptly and satisfactorily from filing through to initial disposal, and then to final disposal after any appellate or enforcement action is complete.
civil law system	The system of law that developed in Europe and that is also known by the terms civil code, European law, continental law, Roman law, or Napoleonic law
common law system	The system of law that developed in England and that is distinguished from civil law systems chiefly by its application of the principle of binding precedent and its reliance on adversarial procedure for most civil and criminal litigation
continuous trial	A trial hearing that is routinely scheduled to occur continuously, i.e., one in which the trial judge or a judicial panel ordinarily conducts the trial in a particular case, and normally no other, from start to closing submissions and with minimal interruptions

court file	A container, often a paper folder, for holding the initiating process and other documents that constitute the court record in a case
court process	A document issued by a court to give formal notification of the making of a court order, e.g., an initiating process
court record	Those documents within a court file that constitute the essential formal record of a case and its outcome
discovery	A formal process by which each party is obliged to disclose to other parties documents relevant to the dispute
disposition or disposal	The process by which a court considers a case to be complete for the purpose of ascertaining the court's active caseload. A disposition can occur by verdict or by settlement.
diversion process	Any non-adjudicative process approved by a court that may have the effect of settling the case, narrowing the issues in dispute, or assisting the court in making an adjudication, e.g., mediation or pre-sentence report
docket	A collection of cases that has been allocated to a judge or panel, to a court location, or to a specific collectively managed case track or stream
electronic filing	Automated processes by which courts accept initiating process and other court process in electronic form using technology such as e-mail, Internet Web sites, or comparable technology for submitting a document and, usually, a filing fee to a court
filing	The lodging of a document with a court that is intended to be included in a court case record or to be used for any other purpose of administering the case
hearing diary	A book or electronic database that records the scheduling of cases before judges and judicial panels at specific dates and locations
initiating process	A document that, when filed with and accepted by a court, constitutes the formal initiation of a prosecution, claim, petition, or appeal for judicial adjudication
inquisitorial procedure	A court hearing procedure by which a judge has an activist role in determining the evidence that will be heard
interrogatories	A formal procedure by which parties are permitted and obliged to exchange written questions and answers concerning the evidence that each intends to use or rely upon at trial
judgment	The formal decision given by a court that disposes of a case. A judgment may incorporate reasons for a decision as well as formal orders.
judicial cadre management	A system of court organizational management under which administrative responsibilities are delegated to judges rather than to non-judicial personnel

Justice Ministry model	A model of court management in which the judiciary is dependent for administrative and budgetary functions on an executive department or other external agency
mediation	Private, informal dispute resolution process in which a neutral third person, the mediator, helps disputing parties to reach an agreement
oral decision	A decision given orally by a judge during a court hearing, whether or not that decision is subsequently put into a formal written form
oral proceedings	A court hearing procedure that makes substantial use of the oral presentation of evidence and submissions by advocates as well as the oral examination and cross-examination of witnesses
petitioner	A person who initiates a civil case in a court for judicial adjudication; also called a claimant or, for criminal cases, an informant
process server	A person, frequently a bailiff, who validly serves court process
register (docket)	A book or computerized database that chronologically records actions filed in a court and significant events in the history of each case
registrar	A court secretary, a chief clerk, or officers with similar titles who may generally deputize for judges in conducting administrative hearings, such as conferences with advocates to settle case preparation timetables
separate branch model	A model in which the judiciary, or part of it, is a separate branch of government and has the same degree of self-government and budgetary control over judicial operations that the executive branch may have over the operations of government
serial trial hearings	A practice by which a court conducts a trial in several stages, each of which is separated by an adjournment
service	The delivery of court process
settlement	An agreement between the parties to a case that terminates all or part of a lawsuit
summons	A court order that the defendant answer the claim, either by appearing before the court at a specified time, or by lodging with the court a document to acknowledge receipt of the summons
transcript	A usually verbatim written record of what is said by judges, advocates, and witnesses during a court hearing
trial court	A court that initially hears and determines a case, in contrast to a court that hears an appeal or a review of another court's decision

APPENDIX B

RECOMMENDED SOURCES

Much of the material that has contemporary research value for justice sector development professionals is available from the World Wide Web and can be found using Internet search engines. The sites that tend to be the most useful and relevant are those of donor organizations, judicial development institutions, and academic institutions concerned with law and justice. Following is a selection of recommended sources, most of which include accessible reports and articles on judicial development and court administration.

GOVERNMENT AND DONOR ORGANIZATIONS

United States Agency for International Development www.usaid.gov	USAID Development Experience Clearinghouse http://dec.usaid.gov
U.S. Department of State – Bureau of Democracy, Human Rights, and Labor http://www.state.gov/g/drl	USAID – Office of Democracy and Governance www.usaid.gov/our_work/ democracy_and_governance
U.S. Department of State http://www.state.gov	The World Bank www.worldbank.org
The Asian Development Bank www.adb.org/Law	Inter-American Development Bank www.iadb.org/topics
European Commission www.ec.europa.eu/justice_home	United Nations Public Administration Programme www.unpan.org
Canadian International Development Agency www.acdi-cida.gc.ca	United Nations Development Programme www.undp.org/governance/sl-justice.htm
UK Department for International Development www.dfid.gov.uk	Australian Agency for International Development www.ausaid.gov.au

SPECIAL INTEREST ORGANIZATIONS

American Bar Association Rule of Law Initiative www.abarol.org	National Center for State Courts (USA) www.ncsconline.org
Australian Institute of Judicial Administration www.aija.org.au/infoserv.htm	European Network of Councils for the Judiciary www.encj.eu/encj
European Judicial Training Network http://www.ejtn.net/www/en/html/index.htm	Council of Bars and Law Societies of Europe http://www.ccbe.eu
International Union of Judicial Officers http://www.uihj.com/index.php?lg=ang	European Union of Rechtspfleger http://www.rechtspfleger.org/ing/ activities_ing.html
Open Society Justice Initiative www.justiceinitiative.org	Federal Court Clerks Association (USA) www.fcca.ws

Federal Judicial Center (USA) www.fjc.gov	National Association for Court Management (USA) www.nacmnet.org
European Association of Judges http://www.richtervereinigung.at/international/eaj2a.htm	Association of European Administrative Judges www.aeaj.org
International Association for Court Administration www.iaca.ws	The European Commission for the Efficiency of Justice (CEPEJ) www.coe.int/t/dg1/legalcooperation/cepej/default_en.asp

APPENDIX C

CASE STUDY SUMMARIES

COLOMBIA

Following the adoption of a new constitution in the early 1990s, Colombia has developed two unique judicial reform programs. First, in collaboration with USAID and other donor organizations, the government launched the Justice Houses program, aimed at strengthening the rule of law in local communities and improving access to justice. Additionally, the municipality of Itagui launched a public-private partnership to modernize the local court system.

The Colombian Justice Houses were established in more remote regions, to increase government visibility in a country that has recently struggled with civil conflict. The houses feature diverse government programming, including human rights promotion and family services. Justice programming is not conducted under the auspices of the judicial system, though the judicial system still benefits. The Justice House programming also includes alternative dispute resolution, legal education, and judicial services to poorer citizens, thus lifting some of the burden from the court system.

Itagui's quality management program was designed to improve the efficiency and performance of the city's court system, provide personnel training, and improve public perceptions of the reliability of the judicial process. The program features private sector support and is partially dependent on local funding. It has succeeded in improving the judicial services offered to citizens, through trainings and new management strategies. In 2005, the Itagui judges received Quality Management Certification from the International Organization for Standardization, an outstanding achievement for any court system. Proposals have been made to expand the Itagui model to a nearby municipality.

EGYPT

While the Egyptian constitution provides for an independent judiciary, the reality is that the court system is subject to considerable influence from the government. The Egyptian Ministry of Justice controls court financing, and hires and fires court personnel based on their loyalty to the executive branch. Military tribunals and state security courts hold the most power, with civil courts often unable to enforce their own decisions. While the constitution grants judges the power to supervise Egyptian elections, in practice, the judiciary is only allowed very limited opportunities to observe election administration.

For the past two years, a civil organization called the Judges Club has been advocating for changes to Egypt's weak judiciary. In 2005, the Club threatened a boycott of Egypt's coming elections if the government did not (1) grant the judiciary full fiscal independence and a status co-equal to the other government branches and (2) give judges full supervisory power regarding elections. The Club also demanded reforms to the judicial pension program and judicial disciplinary proceedings.

Following these demands, protests began, supported by a range of civil society organizations. The government adopted some of the demanded reforms in 2006, while ignoring others. For instance, the newly adopted Judicial Authority Act grants the judiciary financial independence, though the Ministry of Justice still plays a significant supervisory role. So far, these partial reforms have not satisfied either party, and the two sides remain in conflict concerning the future of Egypt's court system.

MACEDONIA

Macedonia's recent court reforms arise from that country's bid for European Union membership. In 2004, the Macedonian Ministry of Justice adopted a *National Justice Strategy*, aimed at harmonizing the country's court system with EU standards. This strategy sets three goals:

- Strengthening judicial independence

- Improving human resources and community representation in the courts

- Increasing efficiency

The Macedonian government and the foreign entities assisting it have largely succeeded in accomplishing these three goals in a relatively short time. Beginning in 2003, Macedonia enacted reforms aimed at increasing judicial independence and improving management. Supervision over the court system's budget was transferred from the Ministry of Justice to a newly-created Court Budget Council, comprised of the presidents of several levels of courts. Staff members in a newly created Administrative Office of the Court Budget Council will transfer some administrative functions from judges to professional managers.

Foreign assistance, such as USAID programming, was instrumental in Macedonia's rapid reforms. USAID contractors trained Macedonian nationals in the mechanics of legislative reform, and initiated court personnel trainings, in order to familiarize judicial employees with the new laws and procedures. USAID assistance also focused on increasing efficiency and improving public perceptions of the court system: in pilot programs around the country, USAID contractors helped improved case flow and records management. Public surveys were introduced, and committees were formed to focus on backlog reduction. Macedonian court coordinators were hired to assist in reforms for the pilot programs.

The National Justice Strategy's goals were largely accomplished by 2006, with marked improvement shown in the performance of those courts that hosted USAID's pilot reform programs.

THE PHILIPPINES

As granted in the nation's 1987 constitution, the Philippines has an independent judiciary. The supreme court is responsible for judiciary branch administration, and supreme court chief justices have taken the lead in reforming the country's judiciary. In 1998, Chief Justice Hilario Davide initiated an overhaul of the Filipino court system. His ideas, along with those of donor organizations, formed the basis of an *Action Program for Judicial Reform (APJR)*, initiated in 2001.

The *APJR* identified the major problems in the Filipino justice system: backlogs; budgetary shortages; the politicization of appointments; dysfunctional and weak administration; and a need to reform court personnel management. To solve these problems, the *APJR* calls for institution building and reforms to court systems management and human resources.

A Program Management Office was created to facilitate the *APJR*'s reforms. This office is solely under the control of the judiciary, and it works with donor organizations to facilitate reforms. A Philippine Judicial Academy was also created, within the court system hierarchy, with the power to train both judges and court personnel. The Academy addresses issues such as corruption, computer skills, and case flow management, training employees as diverse as sheriffs and social workers.

A formal evaluation of the success of the *APJR* is not yet complete. However, shortfalls continue in terms of judiciary funding, and given the large size of the Philippine court system, the *APJR*'s impact may not be as widespread as hoped. Despite these flaws, the Philippine reform attempts are likely to continue to bring progress.

SOUTH AFRICA

South Africa's *Re Aga Boswa* court reform project tackled several major flaws in the country's post-apartheid court system:

Overburdened and backlogged dockets

Failing infrastructure

A lack of public confidence

In regards to the issue of backlogs, several steps were taken to streamline judicial proceedings. In larger courthouses, court managers were trained to oversee administrative functions previously performed by judges. Office managers were hired to handle such tasks for smaller courts. Additionally, some managerial power was devolved from the regional to the local level, in response to a perceived need for a more decentralized administration system. In addition to managers, translators and support clerks were hired. "Nag" clerks are now responsible for ensuring that necessary parties show up on their appointed court dates, to avoid delays and continuances. Lastly, in an effort to reduce the volume of cases on the docket, the South African Criminal Procedure Act was amended to encourage plea bargains and settlements.

Additional effort was put forth to improve public confidence in the South African court system: surveys were introduced to track public opinion, and the new court managers took on responsibility for the upkeep and maintenance for the courthouse and grounds.

Lastly, the *Re Aga Boswa* reforms included the expansion of South Africa's specialized courts. This included training of court personnel and judges for courts which specifically address issues such as white collar crime, corruption, and sexual offenses. The aims of these specialized courts were to increase public confidence and increase the efficiency of the judicial process.